Meet Me in My CAPE COD KITCHEN

Recipes for Seaside Living

Linda Maria Steele

Schiffer Publishing Ltd

4880 Lower Valley Road • Atglen, PA 19310

Library of Congress Control Number: 2015945015

Designed by Brenda McCallum
Type set in Argenta/Sprocket/Times Roman
ISBN: 978-0-7643-4984-3
Printed in China

Cookie Cutter in Heart Shape ©Thomas Klee. Valentine Baking Backgroud ©Pixelbliss. Ripe Blueberries on White Background Close-up ©evgenyL. Empanadas: Traditional Argentina Pies ©zoryanchik. Kneading Dough ©vladi59. Sun-dried Tomatoes ©oksix. Southwestern Black Bean Salad ©fotogal. New England Clam Chowder ©oysy. Slice of Banana Cream Pie©MSPhotographic. All courtesy Bigstock.

Published by Schiffer Publishing, Ltd.
4880 Lower Valley Road
Atglen, PA 19310
Phone: (610) 593-1777; Fax: (610) 593-2002
E-mail: Info@schifferbooks.com

Dedication

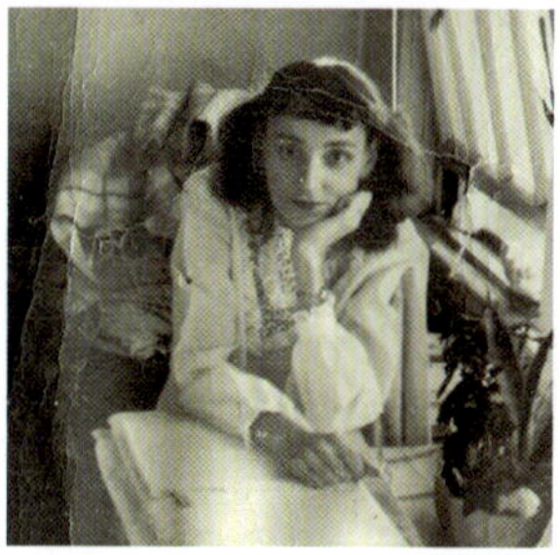

To Lucille Vigeant, my mother's mother, who died when my mom was eight. I have always wondered if my love for baking is in my genes. In my mind's eye, I can see her enjoying herself in her own kitchen years ago, delighting in baking as much as I do now. As my grandfather remarried, I had a wonderful Nana who loved me very much. She wasn't a baker, though she always enjoyed good food and treating us to dinner. She'd buy cookies from the grocery store and pretend they were her own recipe. I always had a feeling that homemade was better. Over the years I have also longed for a family member who shared my interests and was there to pass down secret family recipes. Recently my Uncle Jeff, my mom's youngest brother, located a photograph of my grandmother Lucille. She seems so sweet and beautiful, and I would have loved the opportunity to meet her in her kitchen. I have included her photograph here as an invitation for her to watch over me and my family's kitchen.

Also, to future bakers who didn't inherit a family cookbook of your own, you might imagine what it would be like to "meet me in my Cape Cod kitchen" to bake some of the recipes collected here and create a keepsake for your own children.

Baker's Haiku

Bakers work their magic
In the twilight, dusk and dawn.
Happy bellies everywhere!

CONTENTS

Acknowledgments

Thank you to Nathan, Bella, and Sophia for not only being the coolebst kids a mother could ever wish for but also for being the best recipe tasters a baker could ever want.

Thank you to my friends, neighbors, and family for not only being willing tasters of my creations but also for being such great guests at all those parties and get-togethers. You inspire me to want to cook more and be creative in my kitchen.

Thank you to Ron and Roxanna at the Coonamessett Farm in Falmouth for the years when I was just starting my baking business and for always giving me a place to sell my cookies and cakes in the summer.

Thank you to my mom, the true giver of that Easy-Bake Oven.

Thank you to my friend Mary Kane and to my daughters, Bella and Sophia, for your help, willingness, and support in making the food, creatively setting the table and taking and retaking of food photos. Your creativity and generosity of spirit is greatly appreciated.

INTRODUCTION

When does a love of baking begin? It might just be when Santa leaves an Easy-Bake Oven for you when you're only five. You find it under your Christmas tree, and you wonder if just maybe you've made it to the top of Santa's "nice" list. You tear it open, and use every single recipe before the day ends. You want more mixes. You might even whine and cry a little in the hopes that your mom will take pity on you and buy some more. You burn out the bulb within a week or two, and right before it dies you create your own Easy-Bake Oven confections.

My love for baking didn't exactly stop there. I accepted my first job in high school at a little bakery in my hometown of Worcester, Massachusetts. To me, the bakery was magical. I was intoxicated by the combination of sights and smells of fresh baked bread or large, hot-from-the-oven racks of cinnamon rolls.

The years passed, and somewhere along the way I noticed how much people loved it when I baked or cooked something for them.

Eventually my family and I rented a little house in West Falmouth, Massachusetts. We had access to a perfect little private beach called Little Island. I spent many summers on Cape Cod as a kid, so moving to the Cape felt like coming home. We loved taking long walks on the beach. I'd bake a batch of cookies or pack large slices of lemon cake to take with us to watch the sunset and catch up on each other's day. To me, that first summer it felt like the only thing missing in West Falmouth was a good bakery.

As summer gave way to autumn and my older kids got ready for school, Sophia, my youngest daughter, and I were left with lots of time on our hands. So we'd bake. We baked a lot. I loved our time together. I decided that I wanted to be at home with her as much as I could, so I turned my love for baking into a business, West Falmouth Baking Company.

I began by offering samples to everyone I knew. I gave cranberry biscotti to my neighbors, lemon cake to my friends, and chocolate chip cookies to Sophia's playmates. My neighbor began ordering packages of my cranberry biscotti for her bridge club.

Then I started to receive orders to turn my special sugar cookie recipe into fancy, edible party favors. I'd make whale, sea bass, lobster, and mermaid-shaped cookies as a special homage to the sand and salt air.

I'd personalize the labels to fit the occasion and top the bags with colorful silk ribbon. I loved how much fun it was to be creative with the whole process. I always used the best of fresh ingredients—so the food not only looked good but tasted delicious.

I started to sell my baked goods at Coonamessett Farm in Falmouth. At first I brought lobster-shaped sugar cookies and felt happy when they sold out quickly.

I always added my own creative touch to any recipe I'd try. I've created a number of original recipes including Dreamy Island Cookies, with chopped pecans, coconut, and chocolate, and Celebration Cookies, which are a perfect balance of dried cranberries, blueberries, and white chocolate. Both recipes were inspired by my love for the endless summer days here on Cape Cod. Dreamy Island Cookies came out of a fun day trip I took with my kids over to Martha's Vineyard on the Woods Hole ferry. The idea for Celebration Cookies came to me while watching the July Fourth fireworks one year with my friends and family at Falmouth Heights Beach.

At first, I started to get up extra early to get my baking done while my house was still quiet. My time alone in the kitchen became a welcome, even needed, retreat. I began to feel as if making cookies, cake, and bread was a simple form of mindful meditation. When my oven was on, my heart felt full and my mind empty.

"Restore your attention or bring it to a new level by dramatically slowing down whatever you're doing," says Sharon Salzberg, the famous meditation teacher. This became my mantra.

I began writing a blog as a way to catalog my baking adventures. I added a label on my packages with a link to my site so others could share in my passion for baking.

I wrote *Meet Me in My Cape Cod Kitchen* to put my favorite recipes together for two reasons: 1) I want to be able to pass my recipes on to my children and 2) the best part of a love for baking is being able to share it with others. My hope is that the sharing of my experience inspires readers toward a passion for sharing the joy of making and eating good food with family and friends.

EXCERPTS FROM MY BAKER'S BLOG

I began my blog after I returned home from a weekend retreat with Julia Cameron at Kripalu in Lennox, Massachusetts. I'd read almost all of her work on recovering a creative life and felt inspired to go home and begin a blog as a regular outlet for writing. Food was my passion, and turning to it as my topic for the blog made sense. I am one of those shy writers, but the blog was a fun way to catalog my life in the kitchen, and I knew at least both my mother and mother-in-law enjoyed reading it.

Over time I began to gather additional readers. I posted to my blog for over two years. I have a printed hard copy of my entire blog at home and it's a fun resource to look back on. I leaf through it once in a while if I need some inspiration in the kitchen. Here are some excerpts:

I have been thinking about beauty this week: how beautiful Cape Cod is in the summer, how beautiful my children are and how beautiful something as simple as baking a cake can be.

Both of my daughters, Bella and Sophia, are good bakers too. We put together gift baskets filled with a sample of Dreamy Island cookies, cranberry biscotti and sugar cookies for old friends. We chose a number of moms to send them to—mothers and daughters in Dallas, Texas, that we have shared friendships with. We wanted to let them know we were thinking about them.

I recently baked a cranberry-apple pie, and I realized that I never bake the same pie twice. I always bake it more from what seems most fresh at the market and what I have on hand rather than following a strict recipe.

"If the only prayer you said in your whole life was, 'thank you,' that would suffice."

MEISTER ECKHART

FIVE THINGS I AM GRATEFUL FOR TODAY:

1) My home: especially my super comfortable bed and my kitchen fireplace.

2) Morning coffee: especially when I wake up before everyone else and watch the sunrise while drinking it fresh-brewed with a bit of milk.

3) The completion of my first little "cookbook": it's small but sweet and I created the first edition from start to finish on my own and feel grateful that I did it. I printed copies at a local printer then eventually sold them all through local stores and online through Amazon.

4) Sophia: last night she told me I am "the best mommy in the whole wide world." She asked me if she could find a way to make me smaller so she could carry me around in her backpack.

5) Smells from baking: the whole house smells delicious today from baking cake balls and chocolate chip cookies.

"Be patient toward all that is unsolved in your heart and try to love the questions themselves. Do not seek the answers, which cannot be given you because you would not be able to live them. And the point is to live everything. Live the questions now. Perhaps you will then gradually, without noticing it, live along some distant day into the answers."

RAINER MARIA RILKE IN *LETTER TO A YOUNG POET*

Baking Has Taught Me...

Baking has taught me a lot about patience. I can't rush a good lemon cake out of the oven just because I want to eat it. It will be done when it's ready.

Baking fills my home with the most incredibly delicious smells.

Baking becomes a form of meditation for me. My attention becomes so focused on what I am making that I lose myself in the task at hand.

Baking is both an art and a science. I can be creative and yet I must follow certain baking rules.

Baking is one of those rare things in life that I can be doing and lose track of all sense of time and place.

Baking is something I like to do either alone or with company.

Baking is pure comfort food.

Baking can be incredibly simple—turning almost-ready-to-toss bananas into a scrumptious bread, or increasingly complex—a good New York style cheesecake takes five packages of cream cheese and a half dozen eggs. The oven must be tended to just so.

A note about my kitchen

*"It is only with the heart that one can see rightly,
what is essential is invisible to the eye."*

FROM LE PETIT PRINCE, ANTOINE DE SAINT-EXUPÉRY

I don't have a fancy or expensive kitchen. And yet my kitchen's a very welcoming place. I have a beautiful space because, beyond minor inconveniences like limited counter space, it's the love I put into the food I make and the joy I feel when sharing it with others that brings it to life. It's the many cherished items I've collected over time. Some of my favorite kitchen items were given to me as gifts by friends who know and share my passion for the joy of good food. My good friend Karen, for example, gave me a beautiful ceramic bowl, handmade in Florence, Italy. We've both been to Italy and enjoy swapping stories about memories from our respective trips. When you take the train from Rome to Florence you witness the sunflowers dotting the landscape. She gave this bowl as a gift knowing how much I loved my adventure to Italy. I love to pull these cherished items out not only for a fancy dinner party but also for something as simple as setting out a bowl of fresh fruit for my kids. And my kitchen is always a comfortable place to invite someone over for tea.

For the Love of Cake

Bundt cakes are great because they take less time to bake than traditional rectangle cakes, and Bundt recipes usually produce an incredibly moist and richly flavored cake. They fit perfectly into my white bakery boxes, too, so they are easy to deliver and serve.

Bundts feed 10 to 12 people. In my house, it's more like three to four!

It's fun to bake mini Bundts, too. The pans come in a 48-ounce size, 8-ounce sizes with six to a tray, or 6-ounce sizes with eight to a tray. Bundt pans are notorious for having the cake stick to the pan. The best solution I have found is to generously spray the pans with a quality baking spray, then add a touch of flour, too. Remove the cakes from the pans when they have cooled slightly—don't wait until they are completely cool or don't take them out immediately. Mini Bundts are good because you can easily store some in your freezer for unexpected guests.

Many people have asked me for my Supreme Lemon Cake recipe or my Delicious Orange Pound Cake recipe, and I'm including them here. I hope your friends and family enjoy them as much as mine have.

"Eat more cake. It will make you feel good."

FROM MY CAKE PACKAGE LABELS

Delicious Orange Pound Cake

This cake is very refreshing. The orange juice in the cake gives it a welcoming flavor. The icing melts in your mouth. Try it in the afternoon with a cup of English breakfast tea or as a dessert after a spicy Mexican dish like chicken enchiladas.

Makes 1 (48 ounce) Bundt cake

FOR THE CAKE:

2 cups sugar

1 cup unsalted butter, softened

4 eggs

3 cups all-purpose flour

½ teaspoon baking powder

½ teaspoon baking soda

½ teaspoon salt

¾ cup sour cream

¼ cup juice from orange

2 tablespoons grated orange peel

FOR THE GLAZE:

2 cups powdered sugar

3 tablespoons fresh juice from an orange

⅓ cup butter, melted

1. Grease and flour a 10-inch Bundt pan. Preheat oven to 375 degrees. In large mixing bowl, beat sugar and butter at medium speed, scraping bowl often, until creamy (2 to 3 minutes). Continue beating, adding eggs one at a time, until well mixed (1 to 2 minutes).
2. Reduce speed to low. Continue beating, gradually adding flour, baking powder, soda, and salt alternately with sour cream and scraping bowl often, until well mixed (2 to 3 minutes). Add juice from orange and orange peel. Continue beating until well mixed (1 minute).
3. Spread into prepared Bundt pan. Bake for approximately 50 minutes or until a toothpick inserted in the center comes out clean. Cool 10 minutes; remove from pan. Cool completely.
4. In small bowl, stir together powdered sugar, orange juice, and butter. Drizzle over cooled cake.

Linda's Supreme Lemon Cake

This cake is really great tasting and moist. When friends of ours visited from California I made them this cake the morning after they arrived. They loved it. My friend said that her son doesn't even like lemon cake, and he thought it was delicious. I packed slices for us to take as a snack as I took them sightseeing around Falmouth.

Makes 1 (48 ounce) Bundt cake

FOR THE CAKE:

2 sticks butter, unsalted and softened

2½ cups sugar

¾ cup freshly squeezed lemon juice

¾ cup buttermilk

3 cups flour

¾ teaspoon baking powder

¼ teaspoon baking soda

1 teaspoon salt

4 eggs

1 teaspoon vanilla extract

¼ cup grated lemon zest

FOR THE GLAZE:

2 cups powdered sugar

⅓ cup butter, melted

3–4 tablespoons lemon juice

1. Heat oven to 350 degrees. In a large mixing bowl, beat sugar and butter at medium speed, scraping bowl often, until creamy (2 to 3 minutes). Mix in lemon juice and buttermilk until well mixed (1 minute).
2. In separate bowl mix together flour, powder, soda, and salt. Reduce mixer speed to low and gently add, a little at a time, to butter and sugar mixture (1 to 2 minutes).
3. Continue beating, adding eggs one at a time, and the vanilla, until well mixed (1 to 2 minutes), then mix in the lemon zest.
4. Pour batter into greased Bundt pan. Bake for approximately 45 minutes or until a toothpick inserted in the center comes out clean.
5. Let cake cool 10 minutes, then turn onto wire rack to cool completely.
6. To make the glaze: in small bowl, stir all ingredients. Generously spread on cake as desired.

Variation: For a little different version, you can substitute a package of instant lemon-flavored pudding and ½ cup water for the buttermilk.

Chocolate Lover's Crown Cake

I remember the very first time I shared this cake. I brought it to a Super Bowl party to share with friends. One particular party was held in a friend's "man cave." I felt as if I was temporarily invited into a sacred space. I wondered if the only reason I was allowed in was because I baked this particular cake. At the party, everyone loved how moist the cake was. It looks like it is difficult to make, but it's not. It's really easy. It's a moist double-chocolate cake drizzled with dark and white chocolate. If you like chocolate, this is the cake for you. Kids love to help with the drizzling part, too.

1. Generously coat a large Bundt pan. Break up bittersweet chocolate into a small microwave safe bowl; add oil. Microwave on high for approximately 1 minute; stir until smooth—it may need to heat a little longer. Cool slightly.
2. In medium bowl, mix flour, cocoa, baking soda, and salt.
3. In large bowl, with mixer on medium speed, beat butter and sugar until fluffy, about 3 minutes. Add eggs one at a time, beating after each. Beat in chocolate mixture and vanilla.
3. Place vinegar in a 2 cup measuring cup, then add milk and whisk until blended.
4. Add flour mixture and milk mixture to the eggs and chocolate mixture, alternately, in small amounts, until all are combined. Then beat for one minute.
4. Spread batter into pan. Bake at 350 degrees for 35 minutes or until a toothpick inserted in the center comes out clean.
5. Cool cake in pan 15 minutes. Turn onto wire rack to cool completely.
6. To make the glaze: melt dark chocolate with 1 tablespoon vegetable oil in microwave for approximately one minute. Let cool slightly. Drizzle the dark chocolate in thin lines all over the top and sides of the cake. Repeat process with the white chocolate and place over the dark chocolate. Tip: Use a mini slanted silicone spatula to drizzle. I find it works best.

Makes 1 (48 ounce) Bundt cake

FOR THE CAKE:

4 ounces bittersweet chocolate

1 teaspoon vegetable oil

2¼ cups all-purpose flour

½ cup cocoa powder

1½ teaspoons baking soda

½ teaspoon salt

1½ sticks butter, unsalted (softened)

½ cup sugar

4 eggs

2 teaspoons vanilla extract

2 tablespoons white vinegar

1⅓ cups milk

FOR THE GLAZE:

½ cup white chocolate chips

½ cup dark chocolate chips

2 tablespoons vegetable oil, divided

Layered Chocolate Banana Cake

The combination of chocolate with bananas is unexpectedly delicious. I made it for dessert once, and my daughters agreed it was cake perfection.

Makes 1 (9-inch) triple-layer cake

FOR THE CAKE:

2 sticks unsalted butter, softened

2½ cups sugar

4 large eggs

1 cup sour cream

6 ripe bananas, peeled and mashed

1 tablespoon vanilla extract

3 cups all-purpose flour

2 teaspoon baking soda

FOR THE FROSTING:

⅓ cup butter, unsalted, softened

4¾ cups powdered sugar

⅓ cup natural cocoa powder

4 tablespoons black coffee, brewed (more or less, depending on the consistency you want for frosting)

1. Generously coat three 9-inch round baking pans. Set aside. Preheat oven to 350 degrees.
2. In medium bowl, cream the butter and sugar until well mixed. Add in eggs and beat well. Mix in the sour cream and the bananas, then the vanilla.
3. Blend the flour with the baking soda, then add to the creamed mixture.
4. Spread the cake batter into the pans evenly. Bake at 350 degrees for 35 minutes or until a toothpick inserted in the center comes out clean.
5. Cool cakes in pans 15 minutes. Turn onto wire rack to cool completely.
6. To make the frosting: Cream butter in an electric mixer. Mix together sugar and cocoa and beat into the butter. Beat in the brewed coffee to obtain a nice spreading consistency.
7. Place one cooled layer on a clean work surface and frost generously. Place one layer on top and repeat. Add third layer, and repeat again.

Fabulous Carrot Cake

This carrot cake has been a popular choice for baby and bridal showers. What makes it fabulous is the combination of fresh carrots and spices. It can be made in a Bundt pan, but to really appreciate and enjoy the flavor of the frosting and cake, it is best to make it in two 10-inch rounds and layer the frosting in between. Make this cake when you have a little extra time. Don't rush it. It's worth every last bite. And, if you struggle with getting your daily quota of vegetables, this cake is packed with fresh carrots.

1. Grease well the bottom of two 10-inch round baking pans. Preheat oven to 350 degrees.
2. Whisk flour, baking powder, baking soda, spices, and salt; toss in carrots and set aside.
3. In a large bowl, whip the eggs and sugars together. Mix in the oil.
4. Mix the flour mixture into the egg mixture and blend well.
5. Pour equal amounts of batter into prepared baking pans. Bake 35 to 40 minutes. Let cool completely on wire racks.
6. To make the frosting: Cream the butter, cream cheese, and sour cream. Then add powdered sugar until blended. Spread on tops and sides of both cakes then place one cake on top of the other.

"View from parking spot at MMA"

Makes 1 (10-inch) layer cake

FOR THE CAKE:

2½ cups flour

1¼ teaspoons baking powder

1 teaspoon baking soda

2 teaspoons cinnamon

¾ teaspoon nutmeg

¼ teaspoon cloves

½ teaspoon salt

1 pound carrots, peeled, grated

4 eggs

1 cup sugar

1 cup brown sugar

1½ cups vegetable oil

FOR THE FROSTING:

5 tablespoons butter

8 ounces cream cheese

1 tablespoon sour cream

1¼ cups powdered sugar

Incredible Coconut Pound Cake

If it's possible to be in love with a cake, then I'm in love with this one. I have always been a fan of coconut, and this cake is so moist and delicious. It's also very easy to make. Another passion of mine is teaching, and I am part-time faculty in the humanities department at Massachusetts Maritime Academy. I often bring in samples of my baked goods to share with the department. One of my coworkers wanted to know how I make this cake so perfectly delicious. I tell him it's the butter and the love I add into it while mixing the ingredients. This cake is nice on a summer day served outdoors with raspberry sorbet or with melted chocolate drizzled on top.

Makes 1 (48 ounce) Bundt cake

FOR THE CAKE:

¾ cup butter, unsalted, softened

4 ounces cream cheese, softened

1½ cups sugar

3 eggs

¾ teaspoon vanilla extract

1½ cups all-purpose flour

½ cup flaked, sweetened coconut

FOR THE TOPPING:

Powdered sugar

Additional coconut

---

1. Generously grease and coat a large Bundt pan. Preheat oven to 325 degrees.
2. In medium bowl, cream together butter, cream cheese, and sugar until it becomes light and fluffy, approximately 4 minutes. Add eggs one at a time, beating well after each addition. Stir in vanilla. Beat in flour until just combined; fold in coconut.
3. Pour batter into prepared pan and bake for 55-60 minutes or until a toothpick inserted in the center comes out clean.
4. Cool slightly then invert onto wire rack to cool completely.
5. Dust cake with powdered sugar and additional coconut.

Cookies, Cookies, Cookies

Sophia loves my chocolate chip cookies. Nathan's favorite are my Dreamy Island cookies, and Bella's are definitely my Celebration cookies. So needless to say there's lots of baking of cookies that goes on at my house. There are endless possibilities, and they always taste so good. The basic cookie types are drop, refrigerated, shaped, cut-out, and bars.

One winter I taught a baking class through Falmouth Night School that I called Fun & Fabulous Food. I devoted a whole night of baking to cookies. We made a rolled, a cut-out, and a drop cookie. The class took home an assortment of cookies they made that night to share with their families.

My biggest tip for baking good cookies is to only use fresh creamery butter – never margarine or butter substitute, and be careful not to over-mix the dough. If it gets over- handled, the cookies come out tough.

If you've decided to bake a large batch of cookies, it's worth it to pull out a number of prepared cookie sheets and set up wire cooling racks. I like to use parchment paper on my cookie sheets to keep the cookies from sticking to the pan.

Making uniform cookies is simple. Measure the dough to the same size, shape, and thickness before baking.

When Sophia hears that I am making cookies, she immediately grabs a chair from the table and pulls it up to the counter where I am working.

Surprise Cookies

These cookies are refreshingly good. On a tray, they look like a basic sugar cookie. The surprise comes when you pop one into your mouth and taste the sweet flavor of lemonade. I made these on cookie day during my Fun & Fabulous Food class. I love to bring them to the beach in the summer. I will warn you—it's hard to eat just one. But calories don't really count when you're playing at the beach.

MAKES 18 COOKIES

1 cup butter, softened

1 cup sugar

2 large eggs

3 cups all-purpose flour

1 teaspoon baking soda

1 can (10 ounces) frozen lemonade concentrate, thawed, divided

Additional sugar

1. In mixing bowl, cream butter and sugar until light and fluffy. Add eggs one at a time, beating well after each addition.
2. In a separate bowl, combine flour and baking soda; add to the creamed mixture alternately with 1/3 cup of the lemonade concentrate, beating well after each addition.
3. Drop by rounded teaspoons, 2 inches apart on ungreased cookie sheet.
4. Bake at 400 degrees for 8–10 minutes.
5. Brush warm cookies with additional concentrate and sprinkle with sugar.

Nana's No-Fail Sugar Cookie Recipe

This cookie brought a lot of fun into my baking business. My favorite use for this recipe has been making lobster-shaped sugar cookies. It's a wonderful recipe. It really is a no-fail, roll-out dough. The possibilities for using it are endless. I call it Nana's No-Fail Recipe because my Nana never baked. She would always buy her cookies and pretend they were homemade, but even Nana would be successful with this no-fail recipe.

Makes about 6 dozen cookies

2 cups butter, softened

2 cups sugar

2 eggs

2 teaspoons vanilla extract

6 cups flour

3 teaspoons baking powder

1 teaspoon salt

1. Cream butter and sugar until light and fluffy, add eggs and vanilla. Mix well.
2. In separate bowl mix flour, baking powder, and salt. Add dry ingredients a little at a time to butter mixture. Mix until flour is completely incorporated and dough comes together.
3. Chill dough for 1 to 2 hours.
4. Roll out dough on clean, floured work surface and cut into desired shape and thickness.
5. Bake at 350 degrees for 8 to 10 minutes.

Sugar Cookie Baker's Tip

If you'd like colorful sugar cookies but don't want to frost them, take one egg and beat it well in a small bowl. Paint a small amount of egg on top of the unbaked cookie then sprinkle colored sugar on top. (The egg helps the sugar adhere to the cookie.)

I have made colorful shaped sugar cookies for many festive occasions. You can find a cookie cutter in just about any shape. It may take a little time to find the perfect one, but it's worth it. The cookies keep well in the freezer so you can make them ahead of time.

Once when a friend was hosting a book release party to celebrate her newly published novel I baked her a large tray of red shoe-shaped sugar cookies. For Sophia's fifth birthday party we had pony rides at our house for her friends and I baked pink and purple pony-shaped sugar cookies. When my godson was baptized I baked blue cross-shaped sugar cookies. And when my mom wanted to celebrate her second husband's 80th birthday, she asked me to bake cookie party favors in the shapes of diamonds, hearts, clubs and spades to complement their Vegas-themed party.

Just in Case: Sugar Cookie Icing

I call this Just in Case because I don't like my sugar cookies with frosting. The cookies don't package as easily, although this particular recipe does harden pretty well. And there is always some occasion where frosting your cookies is what is needed.

One Christmas when my daughter Sophia was still in preschool we made a large batch of candy cane–shaped sugar cookies for her classmates. We used this recipe to frost them and covered one half of them with red frosting, the other half with white. It took us the better part of a rainy Saturday afternoon to make them. We put them on a large red and white ceramic snowman platter, and I remember she was so proud to share them with her class. And her classmates loved them. Her friends came over soon after for a cookie decorating party.

Makes 2 cups

1 cup powdered sugar

2 teaspoons milk

2 teaspoons light corn syrup

¼ teaspoon almond extract

Food coloring (optional, if you'd like to add color)

1. Stir the sugar and milk together in a medium-sized bowl.
2. Beat in the corn syrup
3. Stir in the almond extract and optional food coloring
4. Frost cookies when completely cool.

Linda's Cookie & Cocktail Party

One Christmas I decided to host a grown-up version of a cookie-making party. I invited girlfriends over for a fun get-together. I made peppermint-flavored martinis and prepared cookie dough for rolling out, decorating, and baking. Friends took them home to share with their families at the end of the night.

Dreamy Island Cookies

These cookies are delicious and fun. I came up with the recipe after a day trip to Martha's Vineyard with my kids. As we enjoyed the setting sun and each other's company, on our ride home on the ferry, I decided to create a cookie to remind me of our special day. They are a perfect combination of sweet and crunchy with chocolate, flaked coconut, and pecans. Years later, when my oldest son went off to college I called him and told him I was going to bake him some cookies and send them in the mail. I asked him what kind he wanted and he said, "Dreamy Island."

Makes 18 cookies

1⅔ cups flour

¾ teaspoon baking powder

½ teaspoon baking soda

½ teaspoon salt

1½ sticks unsalted butter, softened

¾ cup brown sugar, packed

⅓ cup sugar

1 teaspoon vanilla extract

1 large egg

1¾ cups milk chocolate chips

¾ cup flaked, sweetened coconut

¾ cup chopped pecans

1. Preheat oven to 375 degrees.
2. Combine flour, baking powder, soda, and salt in a small bowl.
3. Beat butter, brown sugar, sugar, and vanilla in large mixer until creamy. Beat in egg.
4. Gradually stir in then beat in the flour mixture.
5. Stir in chocolate, coconut, and pecans. Drop by large tablespoons onto baking sheets. Bake approximately 11 minutes.

The Blue Glass Story

The day on the Vineyard that inspired me to create Dreamy Island Cookies was a lot of fun. We decided to do something spontaneous. We were walking around the Village of Vineyard Haven when we saw an adorable house with a large blue glass collection displayed in the windows. We all thought it looked really beautiful and wanted to let the owners know. We went into town, purchased a whimsical piece to add to their collection, and had the shopkeeper wrap it for us. We wrote an anonymous note letting them know we enjoyed looking at their collection and left it on their doorstep. I've often looked for ways to inspire creativity and compassion in my kids so they will grow up with a sense of empathy. We also visit a homeless shelter each year and donate something like gift cards or warm blankets and hats.

Celebration Cookies

The idea for these scrumptious cookies came to me while we were watching the Falmouth fireworks with friends at Falmouth Heights a few years ago.

I wrote an essay called "The Comforts of Baking" that was featured in *Cape Cod Magazine,* and I included this recipe.

Simply use the first nine ingredients in the recipe for my Dreamy Island Cookies, and follow the first four steps of the recipe. On step five, instead of adding pecans, coconut, and chocolate, substitute white chocolate, dried cranberries, and dried blueberries.

The combination of colors reflected in the red, white and blue reminds me of the fireworks that year. I've been told on a number of occasions that these cookies are amazing. My daughter Bella and her friends say these cookies are the best they've ever had.

Makes 18 cookies

$1\frac{2}{3}$ cups flour

$\frac{3}{4}$ teaspoon baking powder

$\frac{1}{2}$ teaspoon baking soda

$\frac{1}{2}$ teaspoon salt

$1\frac{1}{2}$ sticks unsalted butter, softened

$\frac{3}{4}$ cup brown sugar, packed

$\frac{1}{3}$ cup sugar

1 teaspoon vanilla extract

1 large egg

12 ounces of white chocolate morsels

$\frac{1}{2}$ cup dried cranberries

$\frac{1}{2}$ cup dried blueberries

---

1. Preheat oven to 375 degrees.
2. Combine flour, baking powder, soda, and salt in a small bowl.
3. Beat butter, brown sugar, sugar, and vanilla in large mixer until creamy. Beat in egg.
4. Gradually stir in then beat in the flour mixture.
5. Stir in white chocolate, cranberries, and blueberries. Drop by large tablespoons onto baking sheets. Bake approximately 11 minutes.

Collecting Moments

In this one tiny imperfect life
I've decided it's more important to collect moments
Not things.

Jumbo Chocolate Chip Cookies

Many of my friends say these are the best chocolate chip cookies they have ever had. There is something special and so simple about a really good chocolate chip cookie. We have friends who we meet out on Sandy Neck Beach in the summer. They have an RV they bring for the weekend and invite friends to come and go. I usually bake a batch of these to share after the kids have had fun in the water for the day. We sit on the warm sand, enjoy the gentle gliding by of the boats out in the water, and eat cookies.

Makes 18 cookies

2¼ cups flour

1 teaspoon baking powder

1 teaspoon salt

2 sticks unsalted butter, softened

⅔ cup smooth peanut butter

1 cup sugar

1 cup brown sugar

2 eggs

2 teaspoons vanilla extract

1¾ cups chocolate chips (semi-sweet or milk)

1. Preheat oven to 325 degrees.
2. In a small bowl, combine flour, baking powder and salt.
3. In a separate bowl, beat together butter, peanut butter, sugar, and brown sugar until light and fluffy.
4. Beat in eggs and vanilla.
5. Stir in flour mixture until well blended and dough forms.
6. Stir in chocolate chips. Use a ¼ cup measuring cup to drop rounds of cookie dough onto baking sheet.
7. Bake 15–17 minutes.

Hazelnut Shortbread Cookies

These cookies are super-delicious. The hazelnuts have such a wonderful flavor. Chances are if you've had dinner at our house, I have served them with dessert. My older sister Luci loves these cookies. Luci was named after both of our grandmothers – her full name is Lucille Rita. Lucille was our birth grandmother. Rita was the grandmother who cared for us when my grandfather remarried.

These are easy to make but are fancier than a basic chocolate chip. So if you decide to bake these, your guests will be impressed with your baking skills.

Makes 1 dozen cookies

1 cup unsalted butter, softened

½ cup fine granulated sugar

2 tablespoons pure maple syrup

2 teaspoons vanilla extract

2 cups all-purpose flour

1¼ cups finely chopped hazelnuts

½ cup milk chocolate morsels

---

1. In a mixing bowl, cream butter and sugar until light and fluffy. Add syrup and vanilla.
2. Add flour; mix just until combined. Fold in the nuts.
3. Shape dough into two 2-inch rolls; wrap each in Ziploc bag or plastic wrap. Refrigerate for two hours or until firm.
4. Cut dough into ¼ inch slices. Place 2 inches apart on ungreased baking sheets in a 325 degree oven for approximately 15 minutes, or until edges begin to brown. Remove to wire racks to cool completely.
5. Melt chocolate and drizzle over cookies. Let chocolate set.

Quick Breads

When you live on Cape Cod you most likely have a lot of house guests, people who just can't wait to spend time with you or to be close to the ocean. Whatever the reason, house guests are more likely to head out for a long day of adventure on a full belly.

Quick breads are a great treat to have on hand because they tend to freeze well and stay fresh for days. They also make your whole house smell delicious.

Quick breads are great sliced and toasted with a spread of cream cheese or a drizzle of honey.

Bake quick breads in the very center of your oven. Quick breads usually taste best the day after baking. Never over-mix a quick bread; it can give it a tough texture.

On occasion, I bring in samples of my baked goods to my students. This becomes a tricky thing to do. They love it as an alternative to dorm food and they want me to bring in more. I usually wait until the end of the semester, or if I am sampling a new recipe and don't want to eat it all myself. I remember one time a quiet student exclaimed with a mouth half-full of banana bread, "This is the best banana bread I have ever had."

"The smell of good bread baking, like the sound of lightly flowing water, is indescribable in its evocation of innocence and delight."

M.F.K. FISHER

Pear and Orange Bread

An old friend gave me this recipe. She and I met sometime between second and third grade, and we still look forward to catching up on the phone or meeting for lunch. There's something deeply comforting about being friends with someone for close to forty years. We can laugh at ourselves together and we know all (or most) of each other's secrets.

I shared this recipe in a Falmouth food column when my baking class was being announced. I like to bake it in the winter when I know a friend is going to stop by to catch up. I like to serve it with a cup of hot tea, next to the warmth of my kitchen fireplace.

Makes 1 loaf

3 cups flour

1 tablespoon baking powder

½ teaspoon baking soda

1 teaspoon salt

1 teaspoon cinnamon

½ teaspoon nutmeg

1–2 tablespoons lemon juice

½ cup orange juice

1 cup honey

2 eggs

½ cup olive oil

1 winter pear, cored but not peeled and chopped fine

---

1. Mix gently the dry ingredients: flour, baking powder, baking soda, salt, cinnamon and nutmeg.
2. In a separate bowl, blend well the lemon and orange juices, honey, slightly beaten eggs, and oil.
3. Mix the wet with the dry ingredients. Gently fold in the chopped pear.
4. Preheat oven to 350 degrees and place mixture in greased 9-inch loaf pan. Bake for approximately 50 minutes.

"Never stop doing little things for others, sometimes those little things occupy the biggest part of their hearts."

RITU GABOUREY

Mom's Best Banana Bread

This is a wonderful banana bread recipe: simple and delicious. When there's over-ripe bananas in my kitchen, Sophia will say, "Mom, it's time to bake banana bread."

It seems to disappear as soon as I pull it from my oven. I don't add nuts to my banana bread, but you can. It's really yummy warm with a little bit of butter or even a drizzle of honey. I posted this recipe on my blog when the bread regularly sold out that summer I started selling my baked goods at the farm.

Makes 1 loaf

⅓ cup melted butter, unsalted

3 or 4 ripe bananas, mashed

1 cup sugar

1 egg, slightly beaten

1 teaspoon vanilla extract

1 teaspoon baking soda

Salt, a pinch

---

1. Preheat oven to 350 degrees.
2. Mix butter into mashed bananas in large mixing bowl.
3. Mix in sugar, egg, and vanilla, then sprinkle in baking soda and salt. Add flour last. Don't over-mix.
4. Pour into greased large loaf or several mini loaf pan. Bake for approximately 45 minutes. The loaf is done when a knife inserted in the center comes out clean.

Pecan Bread

I grew up in New England. I was raised in Worcester, Massachusetts, and visited the Cape many times with friends and family throughout my childhood and teen years. However, I spent ten years in Dallas, Texas, with the man I married in the same neighborhood where he grew up. Our first year there we rented what proved to be a run-down, yet charming, house while we looked for a home of our own. The property was long and flat with more than 30 70-foot-tall pecan trees. A train went through the edge of our back yard, and when Nathan and Bella were still in diapers they'd always run to the back of the house to look out the window to catch the train roll by when they heard the whistle blow. I remember one season the trees so abundantly produced pecans that I gathered as many as I could. I shelled and packaged them and sent them "up north" to family and friends over the holidays. This simple and exceptionally tasty quick bread reminds me of that special time I shared with my family.

Makes 1 loaf

2½ cups flour

1 cup sugar

1 teaspoon salt

2½ teaspoons baking powder

1 cup chopped pecans

1 cup fresh whole milk

1 egg, slightly beaten

1. *Preheat oven to 350 degrees.*
2. *Combine dry ingredients.*
3. *Mix egg with milk and add to dry ingredients.*
4. *Let dough set for 10 minutes, then bake in large, greased loaf pan for approximately 50 minutes.*

Blueberry Cream Cheese Bread

I came up with this recipe for my son, Nathan. He loves blueberry bagels with cream cheese, and I decided I wanted to offer him something homemade as an alternative. Fresh blueberries and cream cheese are such a tasty combination in this easy quick bread.

Makes 1 8-inch square loaf

1 cup flour

½ cup sugar

¾ teaspoon baking powder

½ teaspoon salt

¼ teaspoon baking soda

1 egg

8 ouces cream cheese, softened

2 tablespoons butter, melted

1 teaspoon vanilla extract

1½ cups fresh blueberries

1 tablespoon brown sugar

¼ teaspoon ground cinnamon

---

1. Preheat oven to 350 degrees.
2. In mixing bowl, combine the flour, sugar, baking powder, salt, and baking soda.
3. In a separate bowl, whisk egg, cream cheese, butter, and vanilla until blended. Stir into dry ingredients just until moistened. Stir in 1 cup of the blueberries.
4. Pour into 8-inch square, well-greased baking dish. Sprinkle remaining blueberries, brown sugar and cinnamon over top. Bake for 25–30 minutes.

"The Indians and English use them much, boiling them with Sugar for Sauce to eat with their Meat, and it is a delicious sauce."

JOHN JOSSELYN, WHILE VISITING NEW ENGLAND IN 1663

Cape Cod Cranberry Loaf

There is really something to love about the taste of a good cranberry loaf bread. Besides, what would a Cape Cod recipe collection be without a touch of fresh cranberries? I like to add a hint of fresh orange flavor in mine to balance out the tartness of the cranberry. Since moving to the Cape I have really enjoyed the beauty of the seasons here beyond the thrill of the beaches in the summer. The large cranberry bogs in East and North Falmouth and in Bourne in the Upper Cape are beautiful—especially in the late autumn when the sunsets mix beautifully with the bright red landscape of the bogs.

Makes 1 loaf

2 cups all-purpose flour

1½ teaspoons baking powder

½ teaspoon baking soda

½ teaspoon salt

1 tablespoon grated orange zest

1½ cups fresh cranberries

½ cup pecans, coarsely chopped

¼ cup butter, softened

1 cup sugar

1 egg

¾ cup orange juice

---

1. Preheat the oven to 350 degrees. Grease and flour a 9 × 5 inch loaf pan.
2. Whisk together flour, baking powder, baking soda, and salt. Stir in orange zest, cranberries, and pecans. Set aside.
3. In a large bowl, cream together butter, sugar, and egg until smooth. Stir in orange juice. Beat in flour mixture until just moistened. Pour into prepared pan.
4. Bake for 1 hour in the preheated oven, or until the bread springs back when lightly touched. Let stand 10 minutes; turn out onto a wire rack to cool. Wrap in plastic when completely cool.

A Note on Fresh Cranberries

When I was little I remember only being offered cranberry sauce out of a can and only on Thanksgiving. I never tried it back then because it seemed to me like a peculiar food. Years later, after seeing all the fresh cranberries, especially in the fall, and enjoying the beauty of the bogs, I developed a passion for this tart fruit. I now use fresh or dried cranberries as often and in as many ways as I can, such as making an apple cranberry pie, creating a sauce by boiling them and adding sugar, tossing into a fresh green salad, or, of course. using them in my Celebration Cookies and Cranberry Biscotti.

Patti's Pumpkin Bread

I've had a number of friends stay with me who have been so inspired by my love for baking that they've gone home to take up baking as a hobby in their own kitchens. My good friend Patti from California shared this recipe with me as a thank-you soon after she and her family stayed with us for a week. I was happy to hear that her family was enjoying her new-found hobby. Now she shares recipes, as well as photos of her creations and her family enjoying her treats. It makes me happy to see how her love for baking has grown and that she now finds joy in the simple pleasures of baking.

Makes 2 loafs

2½ cups all-purpose flour

2 teaspoons baking soda

1 teaspoon baking powder

1 teaspoon salt

3 teaspoons pumpkin pie spice (or mixture of nutmeg, allspice, and cinnamon)

3 cups sugar

1 cup vegetable oil

4 eggs

1 (15 ounce) can pumpkin puree

½ cup water

1. Preheat oven to 350 degrees. Grease two 9 × 5 inch loaf pans. Sift together the flour, baking soda, baking powder, salt, and pumpkin pie spice. Set aside.
2. In a large bowl, beat together sugar, oil, eggs, and pumpkin. Stir in flour mixture alternately with water. Divide batter evenly between the prepared pans.
3. Bake in the preheated oven for 55 minutes or until a toothpick inserted into the center comes out clean. For best flavor, store wrapped in plastic wrap at room temperature for a full day before serving.

Tip: I remember as a kid my mom used to make similar scrumptious pumpkin bread in a tin coffee container. Simply use a clean tin can and grease the insides. Bake as usual. It comes out really great.

For the Love of Biscotti

I love to invite friends over and offer them a cup of hot tea or coffee so we can catch up on each other's lives. We take a little time to put up our feet while our kids have a chance to play. Serving biscotti is perfect for this occasion. They are a simple sweet treat. They have a long shelf life and travel well.

For years, I didn't even try to bake my own biscotti because I imagined it would be difficult. But after years of buying over-priced and not especially good biscotti, I decided to give it a try. It's a lot easier to bake than you might imagine. Did you know it's simply a twice baked cookie?

When we were still in Dallas, I hosted a literary tea party one afternoon at my house. I invited friends over and served biscotti as we chatted about a book. Since then, I have baked a couple hundred batches. I made chocolate almond biscotti with my baking class, and I have sold cranberry biscotti dipped in white chocolate at the farm and to other local customers.

Cranberry Biscotti & White Chocolate

My daughter Bella loves my cranberry biscotti. I try to keep a package in the freezer, but it always gets eaten up quickly. The biscotti is good dipped in a mug of hot coffee.

Makes 1 dozen biscotti

1 teaspoon baking powder

2½ cups all-purpose flour

⅛ teaspoon salt

3 large eggs

2 large egg yolks

1¼ cups sugar

1 teaspoon pure vanilla extract

1 cup dried cranberries

1 cup white chocolate morsels

---

1. Heat oven to 350 degrees.
2. Combine baking powder, flour, and salt.
3. In a separate bowl, beat eggs, sugar, and vanilla.
4. Add egg mixture to dry ingredients and beat until dough forms; it will be sticky. Gently toss in cranberries and white chocolate.
5. Gently flour a clean, flat work surface. Flatten dough and shape into two 9 × 3 inch rectangles. Bake for 20 minutes on ungreased cookie sheet. Remove from oven and let cool approximately 15 minutes.
6. Gently turn over and, using serrated knife, slice into 1-inch pieces.
7. Bake for an additional 12 minutes or until biscotti turns golden brown.

"Pull up a chair. Take a taste. Come join us.
Life is so endlessly delicious."

Brownie Almond Biscotti

This recipe for biscotti is so tasty, and it is for those who love all things chocolate. It's a fun and fancy way to use an ordinary brownie mix. I found the idea while flipping through a chocolate lover's recipe book at the library one day. I've personalized it to make it my own by adding the drizzle of white chocolate. It's great as a quick snack while out enjoying a beautiful day.

Makes 1 dozen biscotti

1 package brownie mix
(for 13 × 9 inch pan size)

½ cup ground almonds

½ cup flour

¾ teaspoon baking powder

1 egg

3 egg whites

1 teaspoon almond extract

White chocolate morsels, melted

Additional ground almonds optional

---

1. In a large bowl, combine dry brownie mix, ground almonds, flour, and baking powder; mix well.
2. In a small bowl, whisk egg, egg whites, and almond extract. Add to brownie mixture; stir until combined. Divide dough in half.
3. On a greased baking sheet and using greased (or lightly floured) hands, shape each portion of dough into a 7 × 3 ½ inch rectangle. Bake at 350 degrees for 24 minutes.
4. Remove from the oven; cool on baking sheet for 5 minutes.
5. Transfer to cutting board; cut with a serrated knife at a 45 degree angle into slices ¾ inch thick. Place cut side down on greased baking sheets.
6. Bake for 6–7 minutes on each side or until firm. Remove to wire racks to cool.
7. Drizzle biscotti with melted white chocolate and ground almonds.

In My Heart, It's Cheesecake

I've never sold my cheesecake. It was a challenge to keep it fresh and packaged properly. But it still remains one of my all-time favorite things to eat and to make for friends and family after a special dinner at home.

Baking a cheesecake is rewarding because it tastes so good and it seems fancy and hard to do. It's really not. It just takes a little more time and care. It is well worth any extra effort when it comes time to taste it.

Forget about counting calories when it comes to cheesecake. Just enjoy it. You only live once. And cheesecake is worth it.

The very first time I tried a really good homemade cheesecake I thought I might have just died and gone to heaven. It is pure rich and scrumptious decadence.

I remember the very first time I made cheesecake. It was a pumpkin chocolate chip cheesecake that I made one year for our Thanksgiving feast. Everybody loved it. Since then I have made lots of cheesecakes.

Cheesecake should be enjoyed with a good friend. Brew a cup of really good coffee or pour a glass of red wine and invite a friend or two over.

Fancy New York Style Cheesecake

If I had only one word to describe this recipe it would have to be yum! It is so rich and creamy. I will warn you, though; it is hard to have just a small slice. Serve it with warm caramel or chocolate sauce and fresh strawberries.

Makes 1 9-inch cheesecake

FOR THE CRUST:

5 tablespoons unsalted butter

1½ cups cookie crumbs (store-bought shortbread or vanilla wafers)

2 tablespoons sugar

⅛ teaspoon salt

FOR THE FILLING:

5–8 ounces cream cheese, softened

1¾ cups sugar

3 tablespoons flour

Zest of ½ orange

Zest of ½ lemon

5 large eggs

2 large egg yolks

¾ teaspoon vanilla extract

1. Prepare the crumb crust. Put oven rack in middle of oven and preheat to 350 degrees. Stir all crumb crust ingredients in a bowl, then press evenly on bottom and up side of a 9-inch springform pan. Bake until crisp, 12 to 15 minutes; cool on a rack to room temperature (about 45 minutes).
2. When crust is cool, preheat oven to 500 degrees.
3. To make filling: Beat together cream cheese, sugar, flour, and zest with electric mixer until smooth. Add eggs and yolk one at a time, then vanilla, beating on low speed until each ingredient is well incorporated. Scrape down bowl after each addition.
4. Put the spring form pan with prepared crust on a baking sheet (to help catch drips). Pour filling into crust (pan will be full).
5. Bake cheesecake on the baking sheet in the middle of the oven for 12 minutes at 500 degrees, or until puffed.
6. Reduce oven temperature to 200 degrees and continue baking until cake is mostly firm (about an hour). The center will be wobbly when pan is gently shaken.
7. Run a knife around top edge to loosen, then cool completely in pan on rack. Chill cake, loosely covered, at least 6 hours; remove from side of pan and transfer to plate.

Pumpkin Chocolate Chip Cheesecake

Almost ten years ago a close friend offered me this recipe to try because she knew how much I liked ordering cheesecake when we'd go out for dinner together. My first reaction was that it wouldn't be very good. It seemed like an unlikely combination. But I love it. It has an interesting flavor and the chips give it the crunchy sweetness this unique cheesecake needs. Try it as an additional accompaniment with other traditional desserts at your next Thanksgiving meal.

Makes 1 9-inch cheesecake

FOR THE CRUST:

1 cup vanilla wafer cookies

¼ cup cocoa powder

⅓ cup powdered sugar,

¼ cup butter, melted

FOR THE FILLING:

3½ (8 ounce) packages of cream cheese, softened

½ cup sugar

4 tablespoons all-purpose flour

2 teaspoons pumpkin pie spice

1 cup canned pumpkin

4 eggs

1⅓ cups mini milk chocolate chips

1. Prepare the crumb crust. Heat oven to 350 degrees. Use a 9-inch springform pan. In a bowl, stir together all ingredients, then press mixture firmly onto bottom of springform pan. Bake 8 minutes; cool slightly.
2. When crust is cool, preheat oven to 400 degrees.
3. To make filling: In a large mixing bowl, beat cream cheese, sugar, flour, and pumpkin pie spice until well blended. Add pumpkin and eggs; beat until well blended. Stir in small chocolate chips.
4. Pour batter into prepared crust and bake 10 minutes.
5. Reduce oven temperature to 250 degrees; continue baking 50 minutes.
6. Remove cheesecake from oven and place on wire rack. With knife, loosen cake from side of pan. Cool completely; remove from pan. Refrigerate before serving.

What's for Dinner?

When kids are in the house, doesn't it seem like they are constantly hungry? With three kids to feed and who are always looking for something to eat, I have learned to be quick on my feet in the kitchen.

As a baker, I enjoy making things that require a little pastry and some time in a warm oven but can also be served as dinner. During the sometimes dreary and cold winter months, I like it when something is warming in my oven because it adds a level of comfort. The added heat usually extends to the entire kitchen, which helps to take the chill out of the air.

Included in this section are my recipes for empanadas, quiche, two vegetable tarts, and enchiladas.

You can use store-bought, refrigerated pie crust especially when you are short on time and your family is already hungry. But making your own dough or pie crust isn't as hard as most people make it out to be. Someday soon, give my homemade versions a try. You'll feel like a professional, and it does taste better made from scratch.

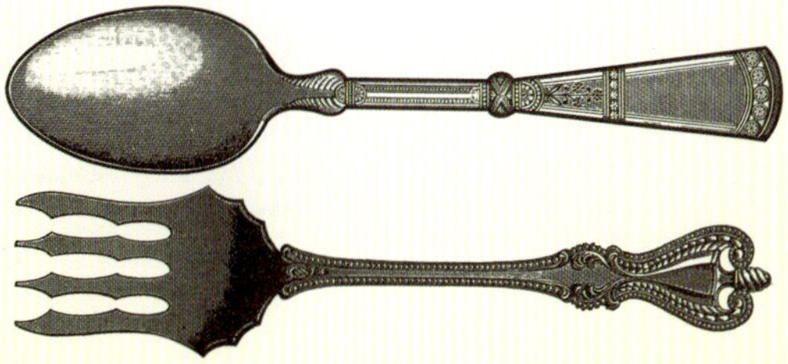

"A meal is the whole experience of getting together and sharing with friends. It is more than food."

JINNY FLEISCHMAN

Peach and Pecan Empanadas

A few years ago I was invited to offer a baking demonstration at historic Highfield Hall in Falmouth. I decided to make empanadas (those tasty Latin American stuffed pastries) because they are easy and people really seem to enjoy making them. The possibilities for filling options are endless. I offered this combination as my favorite sweet empanada option. If you want to turn these into a light summer dinner, you can make a fresh leafy green salad with goat cheese, sliced almonds, and a raspberry vinaigrette to accompany them.

Makes 1 dozen empanadas

Empanada dough and flour for dusting

⅔ cup sour cream

Fresh peaches (soaked in warm water to peel skin, or canned, sliced peaches work well also)

5 tablespoons pecan halves, toasted and finely chopped

4 tablespoons brown sugar

1 beaten egg, to glaze

Sugar, for sprinkling on top

1. Preheat oven to 400 degrees. Prepare the dough (see recipe on page 44).
2. Place rolled out pastry onto floured surface. Using a saucer as a guide, cut out about 8 circles.
3. Place a spoonful each of sour cream, peaches, pecans, and brown sugar in center of pastry. Fold over, and crimp edges.
4. Brush with beaten egg, and a bit of sugar if desired.
5. Place on baking sheet and bake for 20 minutes.

Blueberry & Walnut Empanadas Winning Recipe

Soon after the food workshop at Highfield Hall where I taught participants how to make empanadas, I felt inspired to enter one of my versions into a contest. After using the peaches and pecans as an empanada option, I decided to use fresh blueberries and chopped walnuts in the recipe contest instead. I won first prize and $600!

Turkey and Cranberry Empanadas

My Highfield Hall demonstration was scheduled right before Thanksgiving, so I suggested that finely chopped leftover turkey and cranberries would make a nice savory empanada option. Of course you could use this tasty combination any time of the year. In the summer you can sauté ground turkey with fresh cranberries. Serve with roasted red potatoes dipped in olive oil and tossed with fresh rosemary on the side.

Makes 1 dozen empanadas

Empanada dough and flour for dusting

1 cup sautéed ground turkey meat

Half a small onion, chopped

¼ cup fresh cranberries,
boiled for 1 minute

1 teaspoon sage, finely chopped

Salt and pepper to taste

1. Preheat oven to 400 degrees. Prepare the dough (see recipe on page 44).
2. Place rolled out pastry into floured surface. With saucer as a guide, cut out about 8 circles.
3. Mix onion in with turkey. Place a spoonful of turkey mixture and cranberries in center of pastry. Sprinkle on sage, salt and pepper. Fold over and crimp edges.
4. Place on baking sheet and bake for 20 minutes.

Linda's Favorite Empanada Dough

This dough is so easy to make and work with that you'll feel like a professional baker when you give it a try. I usually throw together a second batch so my daughter Sophia can have fun playing and making her own version of empanadas while Mommy is in the kitchen.

Makes dough for 1 dozen EMPANADAS

1 egg

1 egg white

⅔ cup cold water

1 teaspoon vinegar

3 cups flour

1 teaspoon salt

3 teaspoons vegetable shortening

1. In bowl, beat together egg, egg white, water and vinegar; set aside.
2. In separate bowl mix together flour and salt. Cut in shortening; mix with pastry knife or blender. Make a well in center and pour liquid ingredients into center. Mix wet and dry until dough becomes stiff.
3. Turn dough out onto lightly floured surface. Knead it. Wrap dough in plastic for one hour.

Perfectly Simple Pie Crust

I used to love to watch my Aunt Ollie bring her fresh baked apple pies into my Nana's house to serve with holiday meals. She made making a pie crust from scratch seem so simple and effortless. As a kid they seemed perfect to me. They were flaky and buttery and held the filling just so. She never taught me how to do it, but I thank her for making it seem so simple. Try this recipe with the Spinach Feta Quiche or the Summer Vegetable Tart. Or you can even use it for your next apple or blueberry pie.

Try to work quickly so the ingredients stay cold.

Makes one 9-inch pie crust

1 cup flour

⅓ cup cold butter

3 tablespoons water or fresh buttermilk

1. Cut together the flour and cold butter. You can use a pastry knife or a food processor.
2. When the mixture is blended add the water or fresh buttermilk—just enough so you can form a ball.
3. Chill the dough at least one hour.
4. Roll out onto floured surface and press into a 9-inch pie pan.

Baker's Tip: If you like an extra thick crust, make two balls of dough and roll them both out. Place one on top of the other in the bottom of the plate and with slightly moist hands (either with a little warm water or melted butter) press the two together with your fingers.

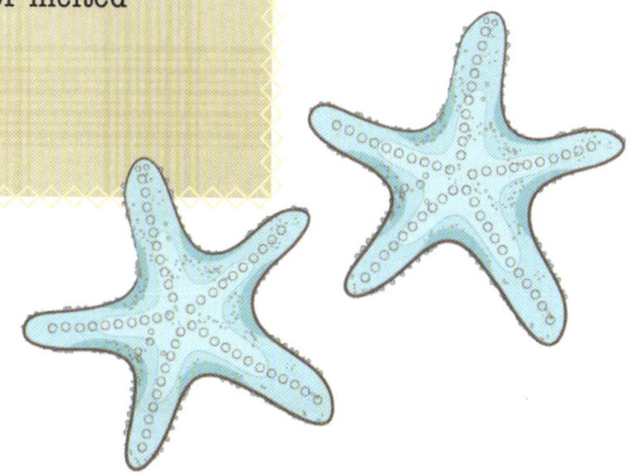

Spinach & Feta Quiche

Even my son Nathan, who for many years disliked anything that resembled a leafy green, has always loved this tasty quiche. It's also really easy. A word of caution: it goes quickly. Serve it warm with a salad or a side of pasta tossed with olive oil, fresh chopped garlic, and pecorino cheese with fresh ground black pepper. I have made this so many times for my family or friends that I make it from memory. It's okay to vary the recipe, too. For example, use Swiss cheese instead of cheddar or jack. You can use sliced mushrooms instead of the tomatoes.

1. Use the pie crust recipe on page 45 or a store-bought pre-made refrigerated crust. Preheat oven to 375 degrees.
2. Heat the oil in a skillet medium high heat, and then sauté the spinach, onion, and tomato for about three minutes or until onions become tender.
3. Cover bottom of crust with the cheese. Spoon vegetable mixture over the cheese.
4. In small bowl, mix together eggs, milk, flour, and salt. Beat well until eggs are light and fluffy. Pour on top of cheese and vegetables.
5. Bake quiche for 40–45 minutes or until it is solid in the center when jiggled.

Makes one 9-inch quiche

PIE CRUST

2 tablespoons vegetable oil

2 cups fresh or frozen spinach, finely chopped

1 small onion, finely chopped

1 medium-sized tomato, finely chopped

1½ cups cheddar or Monterey jack cheese, freshly grated

½ cup feta cheese, crumbled

3 eggs

1 cup milk

3 tablespoons flour

¼ teaspoon salt

Summer Garden Vegetable Tart

I made this for the first time a few summers ago, and my neighbors raved about it. They happened to be playing outside with their kids as it was coming out of my oven, and I cut a slice for them to taste. Not only does it taste delicious, but it is so easy to make. It's nice to have a quick recipe for an outdoor summer dinner and a way to use the abundance of fresh summer vegetables growing in the garden.

Makes one 9-inch tart

PIE CRUST

1 (6 ounce) container of herbed Boursin cheese

1 summer squash, cut into thin circlular slices

1 zucchini, cut into thin circular slices

1 large ripe tomato, sliced thin into circular rounds

---

1. Use the pie crust recipe on page 45 or a store-bought pre-made refrigerated crust. Preheat oven to 375 degrees.
2. Spread the Boursin in the bottom of your pie crust. (Note: you can make your own herbed cheese by bringing a package of cream cheese to room temperature and then stirring in your own favorite herbs; I like to make it with black pepper, oregano and rosemary).
3. Place a layer of squash on the cheese in a circular pattern. Cover with a layer of zucchini and then a layer of tomatoes.
4. Bake for 20 minutes. Enjoy while warm.

Ricotta, Basil & Sun-Dried Tomato Tart

Years ago I included this special recipe in a little book of recipes that I put together for friends and family at Christmas, called Linda's Hearth. I recently dug it out for a fellow writer in my writing group. She had given each of us a wonderful little package of sun-dried tomatoes, and I wanted to return the favor with this scrumptious treat. It slices and wraps well, so it can be a good option for an impromptu meal by the sea when meeting friends.

Makes one 9-inch tart

PIE CRUST

1 cup basil leaves, fresh and gently torn

2 tablespoons olive oil

3 eggs

4 tablespoons whipping cream

12 ounces ricotta cheese

3 tablespoons grated parmesan cheese

Black pepper, freshly ground

¼ cup oil cured sun-dried tomatoes, chopped

½ cup pine nuts

---

1. Use the pie crust recipe on page 45 or a store-bought pre-made refrigerated crust. Prebake your pie crust until edges are golden brown at 400 degrees.
2. Put the basil, oil, eggs, whipping cream and cheeses in a blender or food processor. Season with freshly ground black pepper, and process until just mixed.
3. Stir in the sun-dried tomatoes and nuts, but don't process.
4. Pour mixture into the pie shell, and bake for 40 to 45 minutes or until set. Serve warm.

Squash, Sage & Gorgonzola Tart

I first made this recipe back in October of 2012. It was an exceptionally warm Indian summer kind of day. My daughters and I went down to South Cape Beach and then stopped at Seconsett Island in Mashpee. It's a quick ride from our house, and it's one of my favorite places to get some time at the beach. I spend a lot of time walking there in the fall and spring each year when the crowds are gone. It's a long, wide, open beach with lots of soft hiking trails, too. We walked for over an hour and worked up quite an appetite. I made this recipe that afternoon when we returned home. We enjoyed it just out of the oven with a leafy green salad and warm sourdough bread. I made it again just over a month later to add to our Thanksgiving day meal.

Makes one 9-inch tart

PIE CRUST

1 small butternut squash

2 tablespoons olive oil

1 cup heavy cream, divided

Salt and pepper to taste

6 ounces gorgonzola cheese, crumbled

2 eggs, plus 1 yolk

6–8 fresh sage leaves

1. Use the pie crust recipe on page 45 or a store-bought pre-made refrigerated crust. Preheat oven to 350 degrees.
2. Cut the squash in half, brush with a bit of olive oil and place on a cookie sheet. Bake for approximately 30 minutes until squash is brown and very soft. Let cool. Scoop squash from skin, and place in a bowl. Discard the skin. Increase oven heat to 375 degrees.
3. Fit the pie crust into the bottom of a pie plate
4. In a bowl, mash the squash with a fork, then mix with ½ cup of the cream, and sprinkle in salt and pepper to taste. Spread squash mixture in the bottom of the pie shell.
5. Sprinkle gorgonzola crumbles on top of the squash.
6. Whisk the remaining cream with the eggs and yolk and pour over the squash and cheese. Allow the egg mixture to settle evenly.
7. Arrange the sage leaves in a circular pattern in center on top of the tart.
8. Bake at 375 degrees for approximately 30–35 minutes. Enjoy the tart while it is warm.

Chicken & Sour Cream Enchiladas

This is a super-easy, go-to dinner at my house when we don't have much time, and everyone is home and feeling hungry. Make it to taste and enjoy this easy dish the way that you prefer. We like it topped with salsa, freshly chopped leafy greens, and sour cream, and it's served with chips and fresh guacamole.

I made this for a special celebration for my daughter's fourth-grade book club. We read the young adult novel Esperanza Rising, and there were so many references to food inspired from Mexico that we decided to make this and enjoy it together in the girls' classroom for lunch. They loved it. One of the moms called me a week later for the recipe because her daughter enjoyed it so much.

Makes 10 enchiladas

1 (15-ounce) can green-chile enchilada sauce

10 soft flour tortillas

1 pound boneless chicken breast, cooked, cooled, and diced into small pieces

2 cups shredded cheddar cheese

¼ cup sour cream

---

1. Preheat the oven to 350 degrees. Spread a small portion of the green sauce on the bottom of a medium-sized baking dish.
2. Place a tortilla flat on a clean surface. Place some chicken and cheddar in the middle, then roll up the tortilla. Place it into the backing dish. Repeat until you have used and filled all the tortillas. Spread the remaining sauce to cover all the tortillas, and sprinkle any remaining cheddar on top.
3. Bake at 350 degrees for approximately 20 minutes.
4. Once baking is done, top with sour cream.

Angel Hair Pomodoro

My family has always loved to gather around the dinner table to share a large, cooked bowl of fresh pasta with tomatoes and chat about the good and bad of our day. When I traveled to Italy, I took a professional cooking class to get to know some of the locals. I loved making fresh pasta with tomatoes. When I took my middle child to Paris, France, for her high-school graduation gift, I rented an apartment with a kitchen, and, of course, this was our go-to recipe at the end of an adventure-filled day touring the city sights.

I make this simple recipe in the summers on the Cape often too because it's so easy and fresh tomatoes grow in abundance in local gardens. I love to get out for a run, and this dish is a great recipe for storing up my energy. In the winter, I like to serve it warm. In the summer, I toss all the ingredients fresh into my blender and pulse and serve as a cool pasta dish. Either way, it's easy, tastes good, and my kids love it, too. And making it in my own kitchen always brings back memories from my trip to Italy and my time with Bella in Paris.

Serves 4

1 pound angel hair pasta (packaged fresh)

2 tablespoons olive oil

6 medium-sized tomatoes (ripe, quartered)

2 cloves garlic (chopped)

½ cup basil leaves (lightly packed)

½ teaspoon salt

½ teaspoon pepper

6 tablespoons Pecorino-Romano cheese

---

1. Cook the pasta al dente.
2. Warm the olive oil in a skillet, then add the tomatoes and let soften.
3. Add in the garlic, basil, salt and pepper.
4. Place the cooked pasta in a large bowl and top with the tomato mixture. Sprinkle the cheese on top.

The Art of the Appetizer

One of my favorite things to do is spend a sunny and warm summer day at the beach with my daughters, come home to an outdoor shower, take a nap in the backyard hammock in the warm late-day sun, then call up friends to come over to enjoy appetizers on the back deck. As the temperature drops throughout the evening, we might even build a fire in my back yard fire pit.

In the winter, if we've been cuddling indoors trying to get warm by the fire, we might invite neighbors over for a bite to eat as the evening hours set in. Serving a variety of appetizers is a great way to host an impromptu party without the stress of a sit-down meal.

One of the great things about having neighbors that have become friends when the roads are icy and full of snow is they can still walk over. One year I hosted a holiday party, and I was going to serve a bunch of fun appetizers. I invited quite a lot of people and unfortunately a storm hit at the wrong time and most people called to cancel. At first I was disappointed because I'd put a lot of work into the party, but those who live in walking distance bundled up and headed over anyway and the party was saved.

It's fun to put together a few staples like a bread and sliced cheddar and soft pepper Boursin cheese plate, an olive tapenade with garlic and rosemary flavored crackers, sliced cucumbers and red peppers with a peppercorn ranch dressing, and a bowl of roasted and salted pistachios, along with a selection of other appetizers.

For me, the art of a good appetizer party has to do with serving a combination of warm and hot, meat and vegetarian choices. And to not throw everything out on the table before the first guest even arrives. I like to have one or two staples set out in case someone is starving. My son has an endless appetite and appreciates something to snack on before a get-together begins.

When I was a kid I was always told to wait to eat until the party began, yet I'd feel cranky when it was time to be social. So I've learned to always have food ready from the get-go. Yet it's a nice touch to stagger the food options as guests arrive.

And always take your guests up on any offer to bring an appetizer to add to what you already have. I have a few recipes that I'd like to share with you here that I've served at many informal get-togethers. If I know I'm expecting a few people with big appetites, I like to keep a bag of already cooked chicken wings in the freezer and have some blue cheese and ranch dressing handy to heat up at the last minute. Or in the summer, I like to have a plate of jumbo shrimp with a bowl of cocktail sauce set out over ice and a few slices of fresh lemon on the side.

Baked Brie

I've been making this delicious sweet and savory treat for longer than I can recall. Friends love when I serve it, and you can vary it to your own taste in terms of the type of jelly and nuts you use. Serve it with the kind of bread or cracker that suits your taste, too. Your guests will think you're a fancy cook, but it's not hard to make at all. When my mom and her late husband first tried it, they were impressed at how delicious and fancy it seemed.

Makes 10 slices

1 prepared pie crust
(store-bought or use recipe on page 45)

A large wheel of Brie

4 tablespoons raspberry preserves

¼ cup pecans, finely chopped

1. Preheat your oven to 350 degrees. Place the pie crust in the center of a round baking dish. Place the Brie wheel in the center of the pie crust.
2. Spread the preserves on top of the Brie evenly.
3. Top with the chopped pecans.
4. Roll the crust around the top of the Brie and press down so it folds over and crimp the crust to keep the Brie covered.
5. Bake for approximately 20 minutes or until crust browns and cheese softens.
6. Serve with either croissant crackers or a simple round, thin sea salt cracker.

"One of the very nicest things about life
is the way we must regularly stop whatever it is we are doing
and devote our attention to eating."

LUCIANO PAVAROTTI AND WILLIAM WRIGHT, PAVAROTTI, MY OWN STORY

Flat Bread Pizza

Making flat bread pizzas at home allows for so many creative options for serving as an appetizer. Cut into small wedges before serving. They're easy to make and inspire fun food combinations. Flat bread cooks well on the grill, too. A few years ago I bought myself a new back-yard barbecue and was thrilled to learn there was a special insert that would allow me to make the pizza right on my grill. If you're going to make flat bread pizza for your next party, be creative. Below is a version that I make often, but your options are endless. Get yourself a pizza stone and keep it handy. You can use naan, tortillas, pizza dough, and even refrigerated pizza crust. The idea here is to make it to your own taste and liking. Allow yourself to be creative and explore your favorite combinations.

Makes 6 slices

12 ounces mushrooms, sliced

Garlic-flavored naan

6 ounces crumbled blue cheese

6 ounces shredded pepper jack cheese

2 tablespoons of chilled balsamic vinegar (or to taste)

1. Preheat oven to 375 degrees.
2. In a small skillet, sauté the mushrooms in a bit of butter and freshly ground black pepper over medium heat until mushrooms soften.
3. Sprinkle the sautéed mushrooms evenly over the naan bread.
4. Top evenly with the crumbled blue cheese and top with the jack cheese.
5. Bake on a cookie sheet or on a pizza stone for 20 minutes or until the bread browns and the cheese melts.
6. Drizzle with the balsamic vinegar just before serving.

Spinach Artichoke Dip

This dish is a favorite with my daughters. Bella and Sophia ask to order it whenever they see it on a menu. I've been making this particular recipe for 20 years now, and it's still a favorite when hosting a get-together at my house. My daughters will hover around the kitchen when they know it's just about to come out of the oven so they can eat it up while it's still warm.

1. Preheat oven to 350 degrees.
2. Butter a medium-sized oval baking dish.
3. Mix all ingredients in a large bowl, and spoon mix into prepared baking dish.
4. Bake 25 to 30 minutes.
5. Serve hot with warm, sliced pita bread or crackers.

Serves 10

12 ounces spinach, fresh or frozen, chopped

14 ounce can artichoke hearts, drained and chopped

1 cup parmesan cheese, freshly shredded

1 cup mozzarella cheese, shredded

1 cup mayonnaise

1 teaspoon salt

1 garlic clove, minced

Dr. T's Date & Bacon Appetizer

One thing that can be really fun about living on Cape Cod is people love to host events, serve good food, and be social right from home. I recently attended a birthday party at a friend's house. It's a great spot for a party because she lives overlooking the water on Waquoit Bay near Seconsett Island. I spend a lot of time at Seconsett Island myself, either riding my bike or dropping my kayak into the water there when I feel like going for a ride. She's a writer, too. She was about to turn 60, her daughter 30, and her father was going strong and about to turn 90. He was such a charming and sociable man. He even brought a date to the party, which shows we are never too old for love. The event was celebrated as a 30-60-90 party. Her husband served a fabulous appetizer that to me was a perfect combination of savory and sweet. Since then I've made it at home and my guests love it too.

Serves 10

20 pitted dates

10 slices of bacon,
cut in half to make 20 pieces

Toothpicks

1. Preheat broiler on low.
2. Gently wrap a single piece of bacon around a pitted date and use the tooth pick to hold together.
3. Place on a cookie sheet or baking sheet.
4. Place under the broiler for approximately 3–5 minutes. The time it takes will depend on the thickness of the bacon and how quickly your broiler heats. Watch closely so as not to overcook.
5. Place on a serving tray and pass around to your guests.

Avocado-Stuffed Tomatoes

When we first moved to the Cape, a lifelong friend of mine came down to stay with us for a weekend and we catered the food for another friend's art reception. It was June of 2007. We planned the menu together in my kitchen and got to work making a lot of tasty finger foods we could pass around to potential art patrons. One of the things that sticks out to me about that particular party was this appetizer. It's fresh and light and fun for a summer party. It's also colorful, healthful, and easy to eat and serve.

Makes 20 stuffed tomatoes

3 medium-sized ripe avocados

1 tablespoon olive oil

1 small lemon, juice of

1 small lime, juice of

Salt and fresh ground pepper, to taste

2 tablespoons red onion, finely chopped

20 grape tomatoes

1. Slice the avocados, remove the pits, and place the center into a blender. Add the oil.
2. Squeeze the lemon and lime and add the juice to the avocados.
3. Add the salt and pepper
4. Pulse on low until the avocado is puréed. Add in onion, mix.
5. Gently use a sharp knife to take the top layer of each of the tomatoes off and gently scoop out the inside.
6. Scoop a small amount of the pureed avocado into each of the tomatoes.
7. Place on a serving dish and chill until ready to serve. Insert a toothpick in each before serving.

Queso & Fresh Guacamole

Having lived in Hermosa Beach, California, for six years and then Dallas, Texas, for ten years, I was used to having access to lots of affordable and delicious Mexican-style Southern California cuisine and Tex-Mex food.

One of the things I longed for when we moved to Massachusetts was easy access to things like tacos and enchiladas. So I made a point to make them myself. A great option when hosting is to serve queso and fresh guacamole. It's nice in the summer on the patio with a fresh cold pitcher of Sophia's fresh squeezed lemonade.

I serve queso and guacamole in two large ceramic bowls surrounded by a large tray of lightly salted, thin, tortilla chips.

Serves 10

FOR THE GUACAMOLE:

3 fresh avocados

Juice from one large lemon

2 small tomatoes, chopped fine

1 small white onion, diced fine

¼ teaspoon cayenne pepper

¼ teaspoon cumin

Pinch of salt

fresh cilantro, to taste, if desired

1. In medium-sized bowl, mash the avocados until smooth.
2. Add the lemon juice, tomatoes, onion, spices, and cilantro. Let chill for about an hour.

FOR THE QUESO (CHEESE DIP):

1½ cups shredded Monterey jack cheese

5 ounces green chiles, diced

½ cup half and half

2 teaspoons onions, chopped fine

1 teaspoon ground cumin

½ teaspoon salt

FOR THE QUESO (CHEESE DIP):

1. Place all ingredients in a microwave-safe bowl or in a medium-sized double boiler (see note).
2. Cook until melted and well blended, stirring occasionally.
3. Serve warm with tortilla chips.

Note: Should you use a microwave or double boiler to melt the cheese? It comes down to a matter of preference. For whatever reason I don't use my microwave very often. I enjoy the pans I use and the heat of my stove, but for queso I always just melt it in the microwave. It's up to you.

The Joy of Salad

Summer seems to be all about salads at our house. Whether we start with fresh-picked veggies a neighbor brought over for us to eat because of an abundant overflow from her garden or a simple mix of leafy greens with chopped carrots, tomatoes, and cucumbers or items we picked up from a local roadside farm stand on the way home from a beach day. We make and eat a lot of salad throughout the summer. While we have salad at other times of the year, we treasure the summer sun and the abundance of produce while it lasts, as much as possible.

On days that feel extra hot and humid a large, fresh, cool salad becomes a meal in itself. The abundance of fresh salad options is a beautiful thing. And the possibilities feel endless.

As I've gotten older I've developed a passion for making and eating salad more often and as

a main dish. Salad involves a diverse array of colors, textures, and flavors. Salads at our house include a combination of fruit, nuts, and cheese and an assortment of greens and dressing options. Have fun and be creative with what you have on hand and what seems tasty to you, and turn your next salad into a meal in itself.

"One cannot think well, love well, sleep well, if one has not dined well."

VIRGINIA WOOLF

Black Bean & Corn Salad

I included this delicious and simple salad recipe in Linda's Hearth, the small, spiral-bound collection of recipes I gave to friends and family one Christmas many years ago. That year I decided to forego mall shopping with two toddlers in tow and create something personal from home as gifts. I still hear from friends and family about how they continue to use the recipes included in that collection. I wanted to include this here because it offers inspiration for thinking creatively when making salad and it's also a fabulous simple dish. The ingredients can be easily doubled, and the salad can be kept on hand in the refrigerator for taking to the beach for lunch or serving with a flat bread pizza with dinner.

Serves 4

2 (14 ounce) cans black beans, rinsed and drained

½ cup fresh or frozen corn (not canned)*

Bunch of fresh scallions, chopped finely

1 teaspoon cumin

3 medium-sized ripe tomatoes, chopped finely

1 medium red pepper, chopped finely

¼ cup red wine vinegar

1 tablespoon olive oil

Salt and pepper to taste

1. Mix all ingredients in a medium-sized container with a tight-fitting lid. (Note: If you are using frozen corn, microwave for about a minute and a half before mixing in with the rest of the ingredients.)
2. Chill in refrigerator. Serve chilled.

One cannot think well, love well, sleep well, if one has not dined well."

VIRGINIA WOOLF

Fresh Mozzarella & Tomato Salad

This salad is a long-time summer favorite of mine. It's best when tomatoes are at their freshest. As soon as summer tomatoes are ripe and ready for picking, I can't wait to make this salad at least two or three times a week. I even bring it along to the beach in a container in my cooler. I was able to appreciate the joy of this salad on a whole new level when I went to Italy recently. In Rome and in Florence, the quality and taste of both fresh tomatoes and mozzarella cheese was out of this world. If I'm hosting a dinner party I might make this the way I describe it here, served on my favorite long and thin white ceramic platter with a layer of large romaine leaves set on the bottom, but if I'm taking it to the beach or picnic at the Knob, I might use the grape tomatoes and fresh mozzarella balls instead. One time for a dinner party I used long skewers to hold a cube of mozzarella, a tiny piece of fresh basil and a grape tomato. Then I placed them in the center of a large bowl.

Serves 4

¾ pounds fresh mozzarella, sliced into ¼ inch thick rounds

2–3 ripe tomatoes, cut into ¼ inch thick slices

1 tablespoon fresh basil, chopped

Salt and ground black pepper, to taste

Extra virgin olive oil, to taste

---

1. On a large serving platter, arrange rows of alternating and slightly overlapping slices of mozzarella and tomatoes.
2. Sprinkle the fresh basil lightly over the tomato and mozzarella and add the salt and pepper to taste.
3. Drizzle a thin line of oil over the top. If you're not going to serve right away, chill in refrigerator. Allow the salad to come to room temperature before serving.

Romaine with Roasted Shallots & Pistachio Salad

A friend shared this recipe with me over 25 years ago. It is so good. If you serve it at your next dinner party, your guests will be impressed. It's really easy to make though.

Serves 4

1 head of romaine lettuce, washed and dried

½ cup pistachios, roasted, salted, and shelled

2 medium shallots, chopped finely

Olive oil

1. In a small skillet, heat the olive oil over medium heat, then add the pistachios and shallots. Allow the mixture to heat for 4–5 minutes, stirring occasionally.
2. Place the romaine in a large bowl and top with the pistachios and shallots.

Note: You may not feel the need to use a dressing with this salad, but if you do, I like it with my own version of balsamic vinaigrette (see page 68).

Variation: To turn this scrumptious salad into a meal, top with either tomato/basil feta or black pepper feta.

Summer Salad

In the summer, this salad is my favorite. My daughter Bella and I enjoy making it for dinner a couple of nights a week. And I love serving it when I'm expecting dinner guests. To keep it new, we may swap out the fresh strawberries for blueberries and substitute Monterey jack, Boursin, or blue cheese for the feta or even walnuts or almonds for the pecans. For dressing, we alternate between a lemon poppy seed and a peppercorn ranch dressing depending on how we make it, what we're in the mood for, and what we have on hand at the time.

Serves 4

Romaine lettuce, washed, dried, and finely chopped

4 ounces feta cheese, crumbled

½ cup pecans, chopped

1 cup fresh strawberries, washed and sliced

Sliced red peppers and/or diced red onion (optional)

---

1. Toss the feta, pecans, and strawberries in a small bowl.
2. Place the lettuce in a large salad bowl. Add the fruit, nuts, and cheese on top of the lettuce.
3. Just before serving, gently toss in your dressing of choice.

Fresh Fruit Salad in White Wine

When I traveled to Rome, Italy, I took a cooking class with Chef Fabio. He shared a delightful and amazing way to make a simple, enjoyable, and no-bake fruit salad treat that's perfect to cool down a warm Cape Cod summer day. We used peaches in Rome because they were at their height of perfection, yet, since I like to try variations of new recipes, I suggest using any number of different types of fruit depending on what is most fresh at the market or available to you. I've used pears and strawberries for this recipe as well. A tasty alternative is fresh peaches with kiwi added.

Serves 4

4 ripe fresh peaches, peeled and diced into small pieces

1 cup white wine

¼ cup brown sugar

1 tablespoon fresh mint, chopped

1. In a small bowl, gently mix together the fruit, brown sugar, and mint. Then pour the wine in and blend until covered.
2. Chill for about an hour or so.
3. Serve in small bowls and enjoy.

Chicken Caesar Salad Wraps

I invite my two sisters to come down each summer with my niece and nephews in tow so we can all enjoy time at the beach together. I usually get up early and pack a ton of these easy sandwiches in the cooler. I wrap them individually in aluminum foil and then pack and seal them well in gallon-sized zip lock bags so they'll stay fresh throughout the day at the beach. We eat them after the kids have had fun in the water and jumping from the nearby dock.

Makes 10 wraps

Romaine lettuce, washed, dried, and finely chopped

1 pound boneless, skinless chicken breast, cooked, then cooled and chopped

Salt and pepper to taste

1 cup croutons, garlic flavored

1 cup Caesar salad dressing (more or less, to taste)

10 large flour tortillas (bring to room temperature or warm either in microwave or on top of stove, as they will roll better)

1. Lay each tortilla out flat.
2. In medium-sized bowl, toss the lettuce, chicken, salt and pepper, croutons and dressing.
3. Place a scoop of the tossed lettuce and chicken mixture in the center of the tortilla and roll.

Arugula, Goat Cheese & Pine Nut Salad

Only recently have I been introduced to the joys of eating arugula. I first gave it a try because a friend of mine pointed out that it's not only a flavorful leafy green but also a rich source of vitamins and minerals. Arugula can be sautéed with a bit of olive oil or eaten fresh. At a recent dinner party I made this fresh arugula salad combination, and served it with butternut squash ravioli with mascarpone cream sauce. My guests called me the next day and asked for my recipes so they could make it for themselves.

Serves 4

3 cups arugula, washed and dried

¼ cup pine nuts

½ cup goat cheese, crumbled

¼ cup roasted red peppers

Lemon and basil vinaigrette

1. In a large bowl toss the arugula, nuts, cheese, and peppers
2. Gently toss with the dressing to taste.

Chicken Salad with Cranberries & Walnuts

I love eating freshly made chicken salad. It's delicious in the spring—with fresh fruit and nuts tossed in and not too much dressing—on lightly toasted sweet bread like a brioche. You can substitute a just-ripe green apple diced in small pieces in place of the cranberries. Chicken salad works well for a picnic on a walk to the Knob or a day at the Sandwich Heritage Museum or even Spohr Gardens when the daffodils are in bloom. I make the chicken salad the night before and store it in a plastic container. In the morning, I pack it in the cooler with a loaf of fresh bread. Waiting to put the sandwich together until we are ready to eat helps keep the bread from getting soggy.

Serves 5

¼ cup mayonnaise

1 garlic clove, finely chopped

1 pound skinless, boneless chicken breasts, cooked, cooled, and diced small

¼ cup cranberries, dried

¼ cup walnuts, finely chopped

Salt and pepper, to taste

---

1. Place the mayonnaise in a small bowl and add the chopped garlic.
2. In a medium-sized bowl, gently toss the chicken, cranberries, walnuts and salt and pepper.
3. Fold the mayonnaise mixture into the chicken mixture.

Tip: When making chicken salad, I simply boil the chicken for approximately 12 minutes on the stove in a large pot. Don't overcook, or the chicken will become tough.

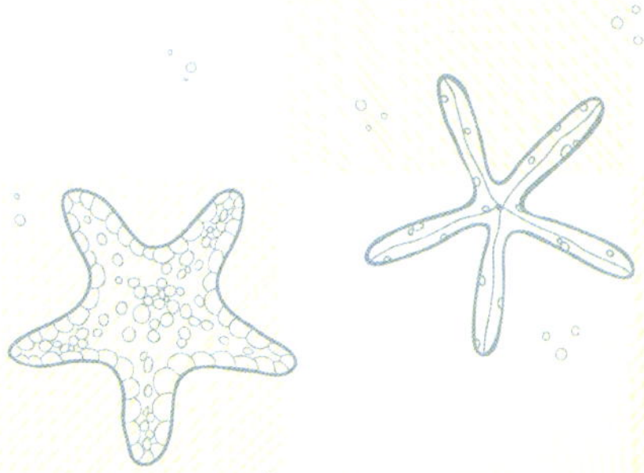

Linda's Balsamic Vinaigrette

I like to make this ahead of time and keep it in a mason jar with a lid in my refrigerator so it is ready to use. It will stay fresh for quite a while, and it's so simple to make. It's a good alternative to store-bought salad dressings, which often have a number of preservatives added, and it goes well with a number of salads. I like it with a simple leafy green salad, a mozzarella and tomato salad and even as a dipping sauce or drizzled over flat bread.

Makes 2 ½ cups

⅔ cup olive oil, good quality, extra virgin and light

⅔ cup balsamic vinegar

3 cloves garlic, fresh and finely chopped

3–4 tablespoons honey

1. Whisk together all ingredients in a small bowl or jar.
2. Chill before serving.

The Abundance of the Sea

Seafood is a light alternative to meat dishes, and when you live near the sea, the options are fresh, high-quality, and tasty. I've traveled all over the United States from Boston to San Francisco and I've traveled from Italy to France, and one thing friends and new acquaintances remark about the most when the discussion turns to food and Cape Cod is the abundance of delicious seafood that Cape Cod is known for.

Seafood is full of protein and healthy nutrients and it can be super fun to catch. There's nothing more rewarding than spending the day out on the water and catching a fish to cook for dinner. And it tastes so deliciously good, especially when shared with friends on my back deck in my own back yard. Whenever I've stopped by the local fish market to pick up something for an impromptu meal, the grocer always has a good story to tell about when and how it was caught. I love to listen to the stories the fisherman have to share about the size of the fish or how long it took them to catch it or how early they set out on the water that morning.

Whether I'm cleaning the mussels my kids caught on an early morning harvesting trip with their dad and his fishing buddy, having a friend over for a lobster roll treat to catch up over lunch or enjoying a gourmet grilled cheese sandwich with a bowl of homemade chowder to take off the chill in the winter air, these simple recipes can turn any ordinary meal into something extraordinary.

Linda's Simple Lobster Salad

One summer I wrote an article for a Falmouth Enterprise magazine supplement that I called "For the Love of Eating Lobster." In the piece, I shared how when we had company visit from Texas one year I served a lobster dinner on my back deck. We ate fresh whole lobster with lots of melted butter and fresh lemon. I collected lobster kits made of shell crackers, bibs, and small butter bowls that I keep in my hutch so I have them on hand for future lobster dinners. What I really love is a simple lobster salad. My Nana used to make us tuna on white toast when we were young, and I've adapted this recipe from her tuna salad.

Serves 4

½ cup mayonnaise, less or more depending on preference

1 large lemon, juice from

Salt and freshly ground black pepper

1 shallot, finely diced

1 tablespoon fresh tarragon leaves, finely chopped

1 tablespoon chives, finely chopped

3 lobster tails, cooked (about 1 pound lobster meat) and chopped for the salad (cooked, chopped pre-packaged lobster meat is fine)

1. Combine mayonnaise, lemon juice, salt and pepper, shallot, tarragon, and chives in a bowl.
2. Add lobster meat to mayonnaise mixture and toss gently until the lobster meat is covered. Chill. Serve on a warm, slightly buttered roll or bread of your choice—a hot dog roll toasted gently under a low broil works well.

Seafood Fettuccini

My Italian adventure inspired a love for creating fresh pasta dishes. And when I think about inviting family over for a summer dinner, fresh seafood comes to mind. It's fun to find ways to bring the two together—fresh pasta and seafood. There are a few good fish markets in town that I like to visit and pick up fresh fish to make this tasty dish as an ode to Italy and Cape Cod. I make it a little spicy for added flavor. Go to your local fish market and see what's on special and freshly caught that day. I make this dish with salmon, halibut, or sea bass. Cook your fish separately, then serve over this freshly prepared pasta dish.

1. Cook the pasta, al dente.
2. Prepare the fish separately from the pasta. You can either grill the fish wrapped in an aluminum foil wrap with fresh squeezed lemon or bake in your oven at 350 degrees for about 20 minutes for an average size piece of fish. Fish can be delicate, so choose a good piece and handle with care when cooking.
2. In a medium-sized skillet over a low heat melt the butter and add the shallots, garlic, basil, and green onions. Allow the vegetables to soften. Toss in the salt and red pepper.

Add the cream and let simmer over low heat while stirring regularly.

3. On a large plate, place the cooked pasta, the top with the cream sauce and fish.

Serves 4

1 pound fettuccini, cooked al dente (packaged fresh)

1 pound fresh fish of your choice (salmon, halibut, and sea bass are nice options)

1 large lemon, juice from (for cooking fish)

½ cup unsalted butter

½ cup shallots, diced and chopped

2 cloves garlic, peeled and minced

1 tablespoon fresh basil, finely chopped

¼ cup green onions, chopped, green part only

1 teaspoon salt

1 tablespoon red pepper flakes

½ cup cream

½ cup parmesan cheese

Breaded Cod Fillet

I love to make this simple fresh seafood dish in the height of summer where it stays light late and everyone is a little sun-kissed from a day outdoors. You can serve this fish recipe with the Angel Hair Pomodoro recipe, or serve it over rice. When serving your fish dish with rice, try my favorite rice dish—simply boil basmati rice, and just before serving toss in finely chopped cashews.

Serves 3

1 cup leftover bread

2 tablespoons capers

¼ cup sun-dried tomatoes

1 garlic clove

Fresh Atlantic cod, 3 medium-sized fillets

1 egg, slightly beaten

---

1. Preheat oven to 350 degree.
2. Make your own bread crumbs by crushing bread, capers, sun-dried tomatoes, and garlic in the food processor.
3. Dip your fish fillets into the beaten egg and then into the bread crumb mixture.
4. Bake for 15 minutes (until it turns a golden color).

"Govern a family as you would cook a small fish, very gently."

CHINESE PROVERB

Steamed Mussels in a Garlic Broth with Tomatoes

Throughout the summer whenever inspiration strikes I'll make this tasty treat. It seems fancy, but it is so easy and tastes out of this world with a fresh baked baguette of garlic bread for dipping the sauce. It's easy and quick, but like all recipes, the quality of the ingredients matters a lot. Buy the best mussels and good sweet butter and use fresh garlic and onions. Figure on a pound of mussels per person for a main course.

Serves 5

1 cup olive oil

1 cup water

1 stick of butter

1 onion, finely chopped

6 cloves garlic, minced

3 tablespoons fresh rosemary, chopped

1 (28-ounce can) tomatoes in thick puree, chopped and drained

¼ teaspoon dried red-pepper flakes

1 pound mussels, scrubbed clean and well, two or three times, and debearded

salt and freshly ground pepper, to taste

1. In a large pot, heat the oil, water, and butter over moderately low heat. Add the onion and garlic and cook, stirring occasionally, until the onion is translucent, about 5 minutes.
2. Stir in the rosemary, tomatoes, and red-pepper flakes. Reduce the heat and simmer, partially covered, for 25 minutes, stirring occasionally.
3. Add the mussels to the pot. Cover; bring to a boil. Cook, shaking the pot occasionally, just until the mussels open —about 3 minutes. Don't overcook.
5. Remove the open mussels. Continue to boil, uncovering the pot as necessary to remove the mussels as soon as their shells open. Discard any that do not open.
6. Taste the broth and, if needed, add salt and pepper.
7. Ladle the broth over the mussels and serve with the garlic toast.

Steele Family Super Easy Clam Chowder

All three of my children have different favorite foods. I tell them I have a theory that whatever I ate the most of when I was pregnant with them seems to correlate to their favorite food. My youngest Sophia loves clam chowder. It's the only soup she'll eat. If she and I are at home on a rainy day, I like to make us thick grilled cheese sandwiches on sourdough bread and this simple recipe for chowder. Treat yourself to this simple soup soon. If it's cold out, it's nice to let this simmer on the stove for the afternoon. We have friends who harvest their own clams locally and are willing to offer some to use for this soup on occasion. But, if we're suddenly inspired to make this dish, we stop by the fish market. There are different types of clams, usually differentiated by their size. Fresh littlenecks work well for this recipe.

Serves 6

1½ pounds fresh littleneck clams, cleaned

2 tablespoons butter

1 celery stalk, finely chopped

1 small onion, finely diced

1 teaspoon sea salt

2–3 small yellow potatoes, peeled and chopped

1½ cups whole milk

black pepper, to taste

1. Place the clean clams in a large pot along with the garlic and water. Steam the clams until they open, about 6 to 10 minutes, depending on their size. Drain and shell the clams, reserving the broth. Mince the clam flesh, and set aside. Filter the clam broth either through cheesecloth and a coffee filter, and set aside.
2. Heat a medium-sized pan over medium-high heat, and add butter, celery, onion, and salt.
3. Add the potatoes to the celery and onions.
4. Once potatoes are tender, add the milk. Then add the clams and simmer until the clams are cooked through, about 1 to 2 minutes for the steamed-open clams.
5. Taste the chowder and add more salt if needed. Serve it hot, topped with pepper, if you like.

Ode to Walking

Sometimes people ask me how I try to stay fit with so much good food around, especially when there's just baked Jumbo Chocolate Chip Cookies or my Supreme Lemon Cake fresh from the oven sitting on the counter. So I tell them about my devoted love for walking. And I feel a book about my life in my kitchen wouldn't be complete if I didn't include my love for walking, and specifically my love for walking on Cape Cod.

I have many favorites but I'd have to say my two all-time favorite walks on Cape Cod are the bike path in Falmouth and South Cape Beach in Mashpee. On the Shining Sea Bike Path, I often park my car in the lot at Old Dock Road in West Falmouth and walk toward Great Sippewissett Marsh (shown here in winter and summer). I usually walk four miles. I often see egrets, herons, ospreys, foxes, rabbits, and turtles, as well as other wildlife and all sorts of interesting plants. In the early spring there is always an abundance of red-winged black birds, and the turtles often warm themselves in the sun on the rocks by the water's edge. The trails near South Cape Beach, between Waquoit Bay and Vineyard Sound, are remarkably peaceful. The walk provides a variety of coastal environments, including a barrier beach and dunes, salt marsh, scrub oak/pitch pine woodland, and "kettle" ponds. I park my car in the lot at the Town Beach side and walk on the path behind the beach front out to the jetty where you can view Martha's Vineyard off in the distance and the backside of Washburn Island to your right.

I was inspired to write the following short poem recently when my youngest daughter Sophia was taking a nap one lazy afternoon as I was waiting for a pie to finish baking in my oven. I first wrote it in pencil on a piece of white paper while I sat at the kitchen table. I still have that original piece of paper somewhere with the juice stains from the berries in the pie.

Ode to Walking

As
I
walk
in the direction
of my
prayer
work
I
am led
to sacred ground.
The burnt umber fields
give way
to
blue skies

Homemade Trail Mix

After a long walk, my kids and I need a quick boost of energy and protein. Throughout the summer, we make this ahead of time and keep it close by for easy snacking. After mixing our trail mix in a large bowl, we keep it handy in to-go portions in bags in the kitchen pantry. Here's an excellent easy combination to have on hand after a walk or other outdoor adventure. Try the one we like, or substitute your favorite snack items for your own homemade trail mix.

Serves 6

1 cup sunflower seeds, salted

1 cup cashews, roasted

1 cup cranberries, dried

1 cup peanuts, roasted

1 cup M&Ms

Thirst Quenchers

There's little that makes me happier than getting together with friends either on the boat, at the beach, or right in my own backyard on the Cape in the summer. After the many end-of-year activities with my kids and my end-of-year teaching each June, we can finally enjoy the back deck, cook something on the grill, and have a fire in the back-yard pit. It's so nice in the middle of the summer when it stays light late into the evening. I never want those kinds of days to end.

Making good food for my friends and family to share matters to me, and just as important is having refreshing cold drinks to enjoy. When the temperature soars and humidity rises there is something special to be savored in making a fresh pitcher of a favorite cold beverage.

There are many alcoholic and non-alcoholic drinks to choose from, and I want to share four of my favorites. Each of these recipes holds a special place in my kitchen repertoire and has brought added fun to many summer get-togethers.

When Sophia invites her neighborhood friends to play in the summer, I love making a large pitcher of fresh lemonade to keep cold in the fridge. When I invite a friend over for lunch, I make a pitcher of Bella's Raspberry Tea. When we are heading to Sandy Neck Beach for the day I'll make a batch of Blueberry Sangria, and when hosting a summer-solstice party I'll offer guests chilled Limoncello.

I love collecting unique glass pitchers to have an assortment for serving and will often stop at thrift stores and yard sales to add one to my collection.

"You never know how many friends you have until you rent a house on the beach."

ANONYMOUS

Bella's Raspberry Tea

As someone who was born and raised in New England, yet spent a decade of my life in the scorching Texas heat, I quickly learned to always have a pitcher of freshly brewed ice tea in my refrigerator. Tea is a staple in the Texas heat. Friends and family there taught me how to elevate the art of making iced tea to epic proportions, from freshly squeezed lemon, lime, or mint depending on the kind of tea we were brewing to loads of crushed ice for a perfect combination of sweet refreshment. Now, when the humidity is high and the afternoon is long, my daughter Bella and I enjoy sharing our backyard hammock, reading a book together with a tall glass of this tasty tea in hand.

Makes 1 pitcher

3 cups raspberries, fresh (or frozen and thawed if not available)

1 cup sugar

1 cup fresh basil leaves

¼ cup lime juice

2 black tea bags

1 liter water, carbonated

Ice (lots of it, and crushed if possible)

1. Combine the raspberries, sugar, basil, and lime juice in a large saucepan. Mash berries. Cook over low heat for about 8 minutes or until the juices are released from the berries.
2. Remove from the heat; add the tea bags. Cover and steep for twenty minutes. Strain, and discard the raspberry seeds and the tea bags. Transfer to a pitcher. Cover and refrigerate until serving.
3. Slowly add the carbonated water to tea before serving. Serve over crushed ice.

Linda's Limoncello

I first tasted limoncello while out to dinner with friends on Main Street in Falmouth. I loved the sweet smoothness of it. It was served chilled in a small glass and we enjoyed it on a patio in the summertime. And I loved the stories my friends shared about drinking it while they were in Italy. They said wherever they went they were offered samples of the homemade liqueur. I made sure when I went to Italy to try it there, too. Soon I invited friends over to make our own homemade batch. We met at my house to grate the peel off the lemons, boil the sugar in water, and, of course, sample it when it was completed.

We had so much fun making it that we hosted a limoncello tasting party. My friends and I made our own batch to share, and we served appetizers. It turned out to be an eclectic party because we each invited our own select group of friends. The party was held at a home on Seconsett Island on Waquoit Bay. We had it in the summer, and one guest arrived by boat from Woods Hole.

I began a new friendship that day with a fun and talented woman who became a cherished friend—an older woman who has sadly passed away since then. We hit it off right away. We shared a passion for writing, Also, I lived in Hermosa Beach, California, while in college, and she was from Manhattan Beach, the beach town next door. She had so much passion for life. She became part mother, part confidante and creative inspiration to me. I hope I offered her half as much as she gave to me.

Makes 1 pitcher

6 large thick-skinned lemons, scrubbed (preferably organic)

4 cups vodka

1⅔ cups sugar

2⅔ cups spring or distilled water

1. Peel the zest off the lemon with a lemon peeler; preserve the rest of the lemon for another use.
2. Place the fresh zest into a one gallon jug or bottle fitted with a lid.
3. Pour in the vodka, and cap the jar. Set aside for three weeks in a dark cool place, giving the jar a shake from time to time.
4. Combine the sugar and water in a pot, and bring to a boil. Simmer briskly for 5 minutes until slightly thickened. Remove from heat, cool completely, and add to the jar, cover tightly, and set aside again in a cool dry place for up to 6 weeks (3 or 4 will do). Transfer to a small decorative jar with a tight fitting lid.
5. Serve chilled.

Blueberry Sangria

When we first moved to the Cape, I was happy a longtime friend since high school already lived here year-round with his wife and daughter. I looked forward to moving here as a year-round resident, too, but I knew it would take some time getting used to and becoming a part of the close-knit community. My friends own a house in Barnstable Village on historic Route 6A and have an old Winnebago they drive out to the off-road side of Sandy Neck Beach. They park it late Thursday or Friday throughout the summer months and leave it there throughout the weekend. Friends come and go, and I've been to many impromptu parties out there. I've made a number of lasting friendships from those all-day-into-the-night trips to Sandy Neck.

I have a large Tupperware pitcher that I fill with a batch of Blueberry Sangria that I bring to Sandy Neck Beach when we go for the day. In 2010, I published my recipe for Cranberry Sangria in the holiday issue of Cape Cod Magazine, and that spring I decided to update my recipe for the summer by using fresh blueberries and blueberry juice in place of the cranberries. It's pretty amazing—and even better shared with friends around a fire pit while watching the sun set at the edge of the horizon on Sandy Neck Beach.

Makes 1 pitcher

1 cup of fresh blueberries

1 orange, cut into small slices

1 lemon, cut into small slices

½ cup sugar

2 cups blueberry juice

Bottle of red wine

6 ounces triple sec

---

1. Stir all ingredients in a large pitcher and chill for at least two hours.
2. Serve very cold.

Sweet Sophia's Favorite Freshly Squeezed Lemonade

All three of my children love a tall glass of cold lemonade on a daily basis in the height of summer. I hang a hammock in our back yard from June until late September. Relaxing there with a chilled glass of lemonade and a good book makes for a perfect, simple, summer activity. Sophia and I like to make this together and leave it in the fridge. I always think it will last throughout the week, yet on certain hot and especially humid summer days it might be gone by day's end. I can see the hammock from my kitchen window, and I love watching Sophia and a friend of hers swing on the hammock together drinking lemonade.

Makes 1 pitcher

2 cups sugar

1 cup hot water

2 cups fresh lemon juice

1 gallon cold water

1 lemon, sliced

1. In a gallon container, place sugar and hot water and stir until sugar dissolves. Add lemon juice and cold water to container. Stir until well mixed.
2. Pour lemonade over glasses of ice, and squeeze lemon slice on top.

"Sharing food with another human being is an intimate act that should not be indulged in lightly."

MFK FISHER

P.S. Poems & Pies

We love making fresh baked pie at my house. I find I never make the same pie twice so I don't write down recipes for pie very often. I simply put in as much of what I have on hand and what is fresh and available that particular season, then fold it into a pie crust with a little bit of butter and sugar and bake it in the oven. We make apple in the fall, peach or summer berry in the summer, and in the winter it's often chicken pot pie for extra comfort. I have a habit of jotting down lines of poetry when I'm waiting for a pie to come out of my oven because it takes about an hour to bake. Last summer when I bought a kayak for us to use, I felt so inspired that I wrote the poem "When I'm 80" while baking Summer Berry Pie one afternoon. I'd been out on the water that morning, and we had an abundance of fresh fruit in the fridge. Summer Berry Pie consists of blackberries, blueberries, strawberries, and raspberries. It's a favorite with my children. They slice large pieces while still warm and scoop vanilla ice cream on the side.

When I'm 80

When I'm 80 I will still want to go out in my orange kayak on the calm water at dusk

so I can catch a glimpse of the osprey return to their nest and listen for the call of the spadefoot toads off in the distance.

When I'm 80 I will still want to watch the rays of the sun dance along the water and peek at the almost

full moon as it rises above the horizon from my perch at the center of the bay.

It will appear as if the sun and the moon are playing seesaw with one another. As one rises the other gently falls.

When I'm 80 I'll still want to dress-up and go out for dinner when I return home. I'll need you to remind me I look pretty even when my hair's turned grey and my skin has wrinkled.

I'll care far less about the laundry getting done and the dishes put away and more about making love in the late afternoon into early evening.

By then I will have grown in patience for traffic, paying bills and putting the trash out on time.

And less for witness to a child who's mistreated or a family who remains hungry.

When I'm 80 I'll no longer remain quiet. I will finally appreciate that my voice when it is carried by

the wind just above the water can not only move me but mountains too.

Summer Berry Pie

This is the kind of pie my beautiful daughter Bella dreams about in the winter when the berries aren't as ripe and we bake cookies instead. It's the kind of pie I like to toss together and pop in the oven while everyone is showering after a lazy day spent at the beach. I may not even know what we're having for dinner yet. But at least the pie is in the oven. When it's baking, the house smells slightly magical. Years ago I was hired for a one-day cooking lesson by a mom who wanted her son to learn how to cook. He'd been watching cooking shows, and she wanted him to have a little guidance and hands on help. Bella came with me that day because I thought since they were the same age it might help break the ice a little. We had a good time and I taught him how to make this pie. They called at the end of the day to let us know how much they loved the pie. It's easy to make. The key is to find the freshest of fruit.

Makes 1 9-inch pie

2 pie crusts

1 cup fresh strawberries, sliced

1 cup fresh blueberries

1 cup fresh raspberries

1 cup fresh blackberries

6 tablespoons cornstarch

1 cup sugar

1 cup water

1. Use the pie crust recipe on page 45 or store-bought pre-made refrigerated crusts. Preheat the oven to 350 degrees.
2. Gently wash fruit thoroughly and pat dry.
3. Place the fruit, cornstarch, sugar, and water in a medium- sized sauce pan, and bring to a boil. Immediately reduce to low heat, and let simmer for about 10 minutes. Let cool slightly.
4. Place one crust on the bottom of a pie dish, and scoop the fruit filling into the center.
5. Cover with top crust.
6. Bake for 35–40 minutes. Cool slightly and enjoy a slice outdoors in the summer.

Ice Cream Pie

Nate, Bella and Sophia's grandmother showed us how to make this tasty treat when we were visiting her one year in Dallas, Texas. It's no secret it gets super-hot there in the summer, and this simple dessert is an easy and fun way to cool off. We make it at home regularly now because the beach and ice cream seem to go hand and hand. It's good for a quick dessert when an impromptu dinner party arises. It's a little fancier than either a dish of ice cream or an ice cream cone, and you can be creative with either a graham cracker or chocolate cookie crust, and the type of ice cream you use. Or you can keep it simple, or serve it with warm chocolate sauce, fresh berries, and fresh whipped cream if you want.

Makes 1 9-inch pie

30 or so graham crackers

1 teaspoon cinnamon

½ cup butter, melted

⅓ cup sugar

A half-gallon of your favorite ice cream, softened (our go-to flavors are peppermint stick or chocolate brownie)

1. Prepare the crust by placing the graham crackers and cinnamon in a food processor and pulse until they are fine crumbs, or simply place in a large zip-lock bag and crush with a rolling pin until fine.
2. Pour crumbs into a small bowl, and stir in the butter and sugar. Use your hands to gently mold together, and press firmly on the bottom of a 9-inch pie dish.
3. Use a large spoon to gently spread the softened ice cream into the pie. Use the back of the spoon to smooth top.
4. Re-freeze. Cut into slices with a pie cutter.

When Joy Arrives

(poem inspired while baking pie)

Joy may enter in on the backs of
angel wings
light as a feather
on a soft breeze
on a summer's day.

She may sneak in
sideways when we
play round robin gratitude
on a cold dark winter's night
on the long ride home from dance.

She may even glide in
on a tall blade of marsh grass as
a great blue heron crosses our path.

When she sprinkles what feels like
fairy dust wherever we go
there is a knocking on the
outer edge of our hearts—
a longing for us to invite her in.

Banana & Coconut Cream Pie

At our house, the combination of a sweet Banana & Coconut Cream Pie is a welcome treat. I like it to make it just often enough so that when I do everyone is excited to have a slice. Especially when some good old comfort food is in order. It's hard not to like this creamy treat. It's super easy to throw together, too. I've had this recipe written on a note card in my file of recipes for years. It has torn edges and coffee stains, but I may have originally found it on the back of a pudding box.

1. Combine condensed milk and water in large bowl. Add pudding and coconut; mix well. Fold in 1½ cups of whipped topping.
2. Arrange a single layer of banana slices on bottom of pie crust. Pour filling into crust. Top with remaining whipped topping. Refrigerate for at least four hours or until very set.

3 Cut slices and top with additional sprinkled coconut.

Makes 1 9-inch pie

1 (14 ounce) can sweetened condensed milk

1 cup cold water

1 package of banana-flavored instant pudding and pie filling mix

1 cup flaked coconut, plus additional coconut for serving, if desired

1 (8 ounce) container of frozen whipped topping; thawed and divided

2 medium bananas sliced, dipped in lemon juice

1 pre-baked 9-inch pie crust

Be Inspired to Get Creative in the Kitchen

Gathering favorite recipes and sharing them with friends brings me a deep sense of joy. It makes me feel like I'm doing something of value even though I know it's relatively small. The way I see it, we all have to eat and it's fun to have a sense of giving and sharing around our favorite foods.

There are certain recipes I look forward to making season after season. Recently the Falmouth food column writer Gail Blakely asked me what I make for Fourth of July festivities so she could share it with her readers. I told her about my red, white, and blue Celebration Cookies and Summer Berry Pie.

Some friends claim they don't know how to cook or be creative in the kitchen without having a strict recipe to follow, and I simply refuse to believe them. We all know what we like to eat, and sometimes figuring out what to make for an upcoming meal can be as simple as a willingness to be a little creative in the kitchen with what we have on hand. It's nice when there's a recipe ready to use and we happen to have all the ingredients, but there's many times when we simply have to make do with what's in the pantry or the fridge for an evening meal.

A simple dinner that's a favorite of mine and my daughter Bella came about because we didn't know what to make for dinner on one particularly dark, cold, and rainy night after a long day and had to use what we had on hand. The vegetable bin was pretty bare except for a single red pepper. There was some freshly grated parmesan in the cheese drawer, and we found angel hair pasta in the pantry. We diced the red pepper fine and sautéed it in olive oil until soft and beginning to brown. We cooked the pasta and immediately tossed in olive oil, fresh ground black pepper, the roasted red pepper, and the parmesan cheese. It was so simple and delicious! Our willingness to be creative in the kitchen is what sparked our idea for this simple meal. It's a quick, easy recipe to make before an evening walk at the beach before sunset.

Creating Community Through Sharing of Food

One of the easiest ways to connect with people or get to know someone more is to share your favorite dish or ask that person what they love to eat. Here are some simple ways to support more community through the sharing of good food:

- Bake your favorite cookie or bread recipe and share it with your neighbors. On the first day of school one year, I gave my kids' school bus driver warm slices of just baked banana bread to celebrate the start of a new season.
- Host an annual neighborhood pot luck. When we lived in Dallas we participated in a fun annual neighborhood event. We shared pizza and beer before setting out for a night of trick or treating.
- Volunteer to bake cupcakes for your kids' school parties. Sophia loves it when I offer to bake for her class party. It always seems appreciated by her teacher and the class.
- Make and deliver a special meal for a friend who either just had a baby or lost a loved one. One of the easiest meals when a friend or neighbor has either just had a baby or a death in the family (and I know they will appreciate a pre-made meal) is a simple baked pasta with cheese, salad, and warm bread.
- Attend local spaghetti suppers and pancake breakfasts. Falmouth has a number of fun and regular events where pancakes or spaghetti are served to raise funds for various causes. It's a simple way to get out into the community and share a meal with others.
- Host a Chili Cook-Off contest of your own. A group of friends attend the annual Chili Contest on Martha's Vineyard each year in January. It's a good time to have a little fun with friends. One year I was inspired to host a Super Bowl party where I asked guests to bring a version of chili and we had a cook-off of our own. It was a fun way to get together. I offered a prize for best taste and spiciest.
- Bake a friend a birthday cake. A longtime friend of mine and I made a pact a few years back that if we didn't think we were going to have cake on our birthday that we had to make sure we made one ourselves.
- Enter a special recipe creation of your own into a contest. A few years ago out of the blue I decided to enter a recipe contest and won first prize. There are many contests looking for the best recipe using a particular food or style of cooking. Enter one of your own creations in a contest soon.
- Invite your family into the kitchen to help you prepare meals. One of my favorite things to do is invite my kids into the kitchen to help prepare a meal. It can be lonely in the kitchen, if you're in there while everyone else either watches TV or takes a nap. I offer them specific tasks to do, and we put on some good music. It has even ended in a number of impromptu dance parties with my daughters

Index

Linda earned her BA in English literature and education from UCLA and her MA in aesthetic studies from the University of Texas, Dallas. She currently teaches courses in language and literature at Massachusetts Maritime Academy.

She is a longtime freelance writer with many published articles. She has written on a wide range of topics from motherhood to grief to teaching and travel, but her favorite topic is food. She also has a secret passion for writing poetry and on occasion she will come out of her kitchen and read recent work at local poetry events.

She has been featured in Gail Blakely's food column and has taught a baking class called Fun & Fabulous Food. Linda loves to invite friends over to cook for them.